Walking
FRODO with

SARAH ARTHUR

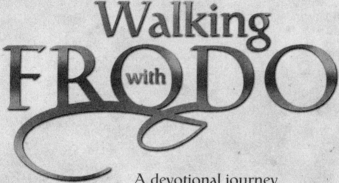

A devotional journey

through

The Lord of the Rings

Tyndale House Publishers, Inc.
Wheaton, Illinois

Visit Tyndale's exciting Web site at www.tyndale.com

Visit www.saraharthur.com to learn more about Sarah Arthur

Designed by Luke Daab

Library of Congress Cataloging-in-Publication Data

Arthur, Sarah.
   Walking with Frodo : a devotional journey through The lord of the rings / Sarah Arthur.
      p. cm.
Includes bibliographical references.
   ISBN 0-8423-8554-1
1. Tolkien, J. R. R. (John Ronald Reuel), date. Lord of the rings.
2. Christianity and literature—England—History—20th century.
3. Middle Earth (Imaginary place)—Religious aspects—
Christianity. 4. Tolkien, J. R. R. (John Ronald Reuel), date—
Religion. 5. Fantasy fiction, English—Religious aspects—
Christianity. 6. Middle Earth (Imaginary place)—Devotional
literature. 7. Fantasy fiction, English—Devotional literature.
I. Title.
PR6039.O32 L6323 2003
823′.912—dc21   2003013922

Printed in the United States of America

08   07   06   05   04   03
6   5   4   3   2   1

For Grandpa, a real-life Sam Gamgee, without whom Grandma "wouldn't have got far"

WHAT'S INSIDE

week four:

week five:

week six:

week seven:

week eight:

week nine:

A NOTE FROM THE AUTHOR

In writing this book I have been wearing two hats.

The first is the hat of literary criticism, which I have worn rather loosely. Among its guidelines is the generally understood premise that *The Lord of the Rings* is not an allegory—with which I heartily agree, in deference to Tolkien himself. Another premise is that it is not a "Christian" story—with which I have some dispute. Certainly Tolkien's story is no more "overtly" Christian than the tree in my front yard; but, like the tree, its very essence points to both a Creator and a Savior, without the need to say so in plain English (or Elvish, for that matter). Tolkien was a Christian. The worldview of any author is evident in his works. *The Lord of the Rings* is no exception.

My other hat is that of a teacher, which is really the hat of a student turned around backward. The way we learn best is when someone takes the teachable moments in our culture and uses those moments to drive home timeless truths about life. Good teachers do this for us because they know that if we are excited about something—if our brains and emotions and imaginations are already fired up and engaged—then we are much more inclined to take ownership of the lesson once it's taught. In fact, the lesson basically teaches itself. We realize, "Oh. I guess I knew that already," though we didn't have a name for it before. Now it rings true.

So it is with *The Lord of the Rings*. To my amazement, my media-saturated generation has taken hold of Tolkien's gift to the world—a treasure both timeless and priceless—and made it our own.

Frodo's story has been so woven into our cultural consciousness that one could argue it is nearly inseparable from our coming of age. And, to my delight as a Christian educator, the story lends itself effortlessly to lessons about the spiritual journey, to the choices we face every day.

Tolkien asserted that his is a story which "is largely about motives,"[1] a point which becomes harder and harder to miss the more one gets into the minds of his characters. What motivates his characters to make the choices they do: devotion to self or devotion to others? To examine this, I have taken nine pairs of choices and used them as windows into the life of the soul. Examples from the story's characters illustrate the "devotion," while the questions that follow seek to apply what we've learned to the choices we make in our everyday world.

I take both my hats off to the many people who helped make this book happen, from my own dear husband and family to my friends in the world of writing and publishing. Without your support, this wonderful adventure never would have gotten past page one.

And to my readers I say, as Gandalf said to Pippin, "If you have walked all these days with closed ears and mind asleep, wake up now!"[2] Frodo is leaving the front door of Bag End. Will you walk with him?

Sarah Arthur

READ THIS FIRST

Fantasy literature is suddenly cool, thanks to *The Lord of the Rings*. And we're not talking about the fluffy stuff, either (in which Benji the Brave raises the Horn of Ippydoo to call forth the god Mork during the Age before People Knew How to Tell Time). No, we want *the good stuff*. We want cosmic battles between the forces of light and darkness, battles in which all the peace-loving people of the earth must band together or be lost to oblivion. We want interesting characters who face the threat of annihilation bravely—and die well. We want suspense, action, romance, and hard-won happy endings.

If we're honest, we want life itself to be that way. Deep down we suspect that it is. But on the surface, it looks . . . well . . . fluffy. For example, those are *not* Orcs approaching us in the cafeteria, telling us we're sitting at *their* table. They're just big guys in jerseys whose grandmothers probably love them dearly and wish they would brush their teeth more often. Those are *not* Wizards teaching our advanced algebra classes. They're just middle-aged folks in street clothes whose biggest battle with the forces of darkness is trying to get us to memorize the quadratic formula. We ourselves are not Elves, or Dwarves, or even Hobbits (although some of us are still growing into our feet). We're just ordinary people who want life to be more than just homework and dating and going somewhere warm for spring break.

But don't be fooled. Life *is* more than fluff. Underneath the crust of our existence is a battle between the forces of good and evil, a battle that began at the dawn of time and will continue to the last age of the world. We catch glimpses of that evil whenever our parents start screaming at each other. Or whenever a friend goes off the deep end. Or whenever a temptation becomes too strong to resist. We strongly suspect it when a relative calls to say he's dying of cancer. And we come face-to-face with it when commercial airplanes filled with passengers are deliberately flown into skyscrapers and life as we know it changes forever.

Yet we catch glimpses of good, too: the kindness of a stranger, a heartening victory over some addiction, the little bits of grace or healing or laughter in our darkest moments. We are able to look back on those times and discover that—had things not happened in just a certain way, bad as they were—the whole situation would have been a lot worse. And even if we fail to see it just yet—even if the future looks just as grim as the past—we have the promise that the Author of the Story has planned a happy ending beyond our wildest hopes.

This is the profound truth behind *The Lord of the Rings.* This is what makes it *the good stuff.* J. R. R. Tolkien was not trying to tell us that our schoolmates are actually Orcs in disguise or that our teachers fight Balrogs in their spare time. In fact, he was just trying to tell us a good story. But Tolkien did have a set of beliefs that colored and shaped his story and gave it meaning (every writer does). That's where *the good stuff* comes from.

So what were those beliefs?

Tolkien was a Christian. This is clear from his other writings and from the testimonies of people who knew him. Christians believe that not only is *the good stuff* real, but it's made possible through Jesus Christ. But Jesus is more than just the corporate sponsor ("This Life Is Brought to You by . . ."). He's the Author of the story of life itself, who jumped in and became a central character just in time to save the day.

In that respect, you might say that Jesus, like Gandalf, is the Savior: He has fought the powers of hell on our behalf and returned from the dead in order to save us in our darkest hour of need. And Jesus, like Aragorn, is the King: He is the rightful heir to the throne of our hearts, the One who deserves our allegiance and service forever. So each of us, like Frodo, is faced with a choice: to humbly persevere in the tasks our Savior-King has chosen for us to do, or to slowly succumb to the darkness.

In this book we'll look at a host of characters from *The Lord of the Rings* who face choices in the ongoing battle between light and darkness. We'll explore what motivates them to make the choices they do: Is it devotion to self or devotion to others? We'll discuss the outcome of their decisions and the timeless truths they have to teach us. Then we'll look to the Bible to give us the spiritual roots for those truths. And finally, we'll ask tough questions that help us apply those truths to everyday life. In other words, what does this have to do with school? with my friends? with getting along with my parents? and so on.

One of Jesus' best friends wrote, "If we claim to have fellowship with him yet walk in the darkness, we lie and do not live by the truth. But if we walk in the light, as he is in the light, we have fellowship with one another, and the blood of Jesus, his Son, purifies us from all sin" (1 John 1:6-7).

Now that's *the good stuff!*

how to use this book

This book is intended to be a devotional guide. That means there are short readings based on themes in *The Lord of the Rings,* followed by related Bible passages and "Going Further" questions for reflection. You will want to *(a)* be familiar with the movies or the books, *(b)* have a Bible handy, and *(c)* grab a pen or pencil. Keep in mind there will be times when the devotions refer to things that happened in the books and times when they refer to things that happened in the movies, but generally speaking the references are to both. For those who have never read the books, the "Quick Reference Guide" in the back can help you keep track of who is who and what is what in *Walking with Frodo*.

The eighteen devotions in this book are actually nine pairs (nine being a rather *LOTR*-friendly number, don't you think?). Each pair explores two different ways to react in a given situation, e.g., Will you choose deceit or honesty? The first devotion in the pair examines our tendency to serve ourselves; the second looks at our call to serve God and others. Each ends with a challenge: How will you make this truth practical in your daily life?

In other words, what are you going to do about it?

GOING FURTHER:

What's your favorite part of *The Lord of the Rings?*

The fact that no matter what happens, the friends are always there for each other.

What makes it *the good stuff?*

It makes us believe that we can triumph over the most evil things w/ help.

What evidence do you see of the battle between good and evil in our world?

jealousy, animosity

everything that gets in the way

WEEK ONE

CHOOSING
DARKNESS
or
LIGHT

Part One:

choosing darkness

The Balrog made no answer. The fire in it seemed to die,
but the darkness grew.

—From *The Fellowship of the Ring*, Book Two, Chapter Five

Think back to the opening night of *The Two
Towers*.

Your *LOTR*-junkie friends have just stood in line for six hours to buy tickets. They now hand you a ticket in exchange for several buckets of movie popcorn (it occurs to you later that they had the better deal), predicting in low tones that madness will erupt the instant the theater opens. But this is something you have anticipated and trained for together. Your plan:

Step #1: Lock arms.

Step #2: Mosh. If that fails:

Step #3: Bodysurf to the eighth row (middle seat) and hold fast till the others arrive.

The training pays off. You storm the doors and seize the eighth row, popcorn miraculously intact. After arm-wrestling a couple of junior high kids into submission, you and your friends get comfortably seated. The movie won't start for another hour, but what's one hour? You've been waiting a whole year.

Just when you've decided that you desperately need to go to the bathroom, the lights dim and the action begins. You've talked about this for months, but nothing in your wildest dreams has prepared you for the stomach-lurching shot over the mountains into the Mines of Moria; and nothing has prepared you for Gandalf's epic struggle with the Balrog, falling headfirst down the abyss.

How on earth did those CGI[3] guys *do* it?

But most importantly, how does *Gandalf* do it?

In the previous flick, Gandalf stands on the bridge looking small and frail against the looming giant of a whip-cracking Balrog. You can hardly believe that Gandalf will survive the fall into the abyss, let alone everything that happens afterwards. But you have read the books (after all, you and your friends are *LOTR* junkies). And you know the nightmare has only just begun.

The Balrog is portrayed in the movie as a creature of fire and flame. Tolkien also presents it as a creature of darkness—one of many—and not the darkest of the dark, either (don't forget Shelob). In *The Fellowship of the Ring* Tolkien writes,

> What it was could not be seen: it was like a great shadow, in the middle of which was a dark form, of man-shape maybe, yet greater; and a power and terror seemed to be in it and to go before it.[4]

The idea that darkness would present itself as a *being*—with not only a visible form but also an intellect and will—is terrifying. When this being first appears in *The Fellowship of the Ring*, there is instant panic among the members of the Fellowship. It's like they've suddenly been struck blind with fear, confusion, and despair. Such an encounter is more than any of them bargained for in this journey they agreed to take with Frodo, a kind of nightmare that surpasses anything Frodo himself could have imagined before leaving the front door of Bag End. Aragorn and Boromir beg to fight the creature, but Gandalf says, "Fly! This is a foe beyond any of you."[5] In the end, only Gandalf stands fast, and it costs him everything.

So here's the point.

There *is* such a being, though he may not have a visible form like what Tolkien or the *LOTR* movie gurus created. (In fact, C. S. Lewis, author of *The Screwtape Letters*, pictured him dressed in a business suit.) And the analogy is far from perfect.

But he's real.

At the heart of the spiritual opposition to the Creator God of the universe is a character who goes by many names: Satan, Beelzebub, the devil, the enemy, the evil one. Satan was once an angel who rebelled against God. He fled from the light of God's presence to establish his own throne in darkness, taking a host of rebellious angels with him (Jude 1:6). Jesus said of him, "I saw Satan fall like lightning from heaven" (Luke 10:18). Satan has been waging war with God and all who belong to him ever since.

Whatever the murky history of his past, Satan is real. He specializes in absorbing light, in casting shadows, and in generating great vacuums of fear and spiritual blindness. He is especially good at blocking the way of those who have sworn allegiance to Jesus Christ and at stopping them from accomplishing whatever tasks God has given them to do (1 Peter 5:8-9). He has also mastered the art of convincing people that he doesn't exist, that there's no such thing as darkness (Isaiah 5:20). And he takes particular delight in enslaving people to the darkness before they have a chance to love the Light, by teaching them to hate the Light itself (John 3:19-20).

This is the lesson of the Balrog from deep within the heart of Moria:

James
1:2-6

YOU ARE SMALL.
YOUR FOE IS BIG.

So what are you going to do about it?

For our struggle is not against flesh and blood, but against the rulers, against the authorities, against the powers of this dark world and against the spiritual forces of evil in the heavenly realms.
EPHESIANS 6:12

THE WORD ON DARKNESS

Take some time to read one or more of the following Bible passages:
Isaiah 5:20; John 3:19-20; 1 Peter 5:8-9

GOING FURTHER:

What evidence do you see of the power of darkness at work in your world? *doubters, the utter lack of responsibility in this time in our lives*

Who among your friends or family is ignoring this reality? *I don't know, we all seem to want to ignore it at some point*

Who has given in to paralysis, despair, or exhaustion in the face of darkness? *all of us, at some point. It's hard to put doubt aside for faith.*

Who actually likes the darkness and hates the Light? *It's easier at points in our lives to like the darkness. It doesn't take any work.*

What about you: What is your response to the darkness? *I am trying to fight despair and doubt. Darkness can keep bringing to doubt and fear myself*

What are you going to do about it?

keep studying and holding to something stable

Part Two:

CHOOSING LIGHT

But still Gandalf could be seen, glimmering in the gloom;
he seemed small, and altogether alone: grey and bent, like
a wizened tree before the onset of a storm.

—FROM *THE FELLOWSHIP OF THE RING*, BOOK TWO, CHAPTER FIVE

How *does* Gandalf do it?

The Fellowship is on the run, the Balrog in full chase. Even the Orcs have fled in terror. Gimli has been "tossed" across the chasm just in time; the others are quickly giving in to fear. As Frodo recovers from his second near-fatal blow of the journey, those who have pledged to walk with him find themselves racing through passageways and down the stairs toward the Bridge of Khazad-dûm with only one thought: *Survive.*

They clear the bridge just as the Balrog appears. And before they know what is happening, their leader has turned and barred its way. This wizened old man, with a face like the nicest of Santa Clauses, plants his staff on the bridge and announces, "You cannot pass. . . . I am a servant of the Secret Fire, wielder of the flame of Anor. You cannot pass. The dark fire will not avail you, flame of Udûn. Go back to the Shadow!"[6]

Dude, you think. *This is one cool grandpa.*

They duel. In a matter of cinematic seconds, the bridge is busted in half and the Balrog crashes into the abyss. There is a collective sigh of relief. Even Gandalf turns to leave, exhausted. But then comes the whip, flinging up for one last time, and down he goes.

After this tragedy, the Fellowship has no hope of seeing Gandalf again. Aragorn says, "Farewell, Gandalf! . . . What hope have we without you?"[7] They never even consider that this wizard, whom they know so little about, is a person far greater and far more powerful than any of them could have guessed. They know only themselves and their own strength: none of them could have survived such a fall. It isn't until Gandalf appears before them in the forest of Fangorn, blazing with light and altered beyond immediate recognition, that they finally get it: The war against the advancing darkness *can* be won. But only through a power and a light greater than themselves.

This is the point:

YOU ARE SMALL. YOUR
FOE IS BIG. BUT YOUR
GOD IS BIGGER STILL.

Even so, you are like a candle without a flame. It is impossible to light yourself.

Jesus said, "I am the light of the world. Whoever follows me will never walk in darkness, but will have the light of life" (John 8:12). Having heard it put so bluntly, it's a wonder that his friends didn't understand him. They were like the Fellowship following Gandalf through the Mines. Even though they followed Jesus for three years, watching him perform miracles and raise the dead and send demons squealing back to the darkness, they never

guessed that their leader and friend was God himself, that Jesus was—and *is*—Light personified.

They watched in terror and helplessness as Jesus
was crucified, recalling later that "darkness came
over the whole land until the ninth hour, for the
sun stopped shining" (Luke 23:44-45). They
grieved the loss, probably wondering, "What hope
have we without him?" There was nothing but
darkness on the horizon of the future, now that the
Light had gone out of the world.

But then came Easter. In the early dawn hours of
that day, as the disciples huddled together in fear,
an extraordinary thing happened. The impossible
became possible. The stuff of stories came crash-
ing into the real world. Jesus returned, just as he
promised—like Gandalf on the hilltop above
Helm's Deep, like Aragorn sailing down the
Anduin, like the Eagles winging to the foot of
Mount Doom at the last possible moment. Darkness was defeated once and for all.

What happened to Jesus in those dark hours between the time of his death and the moment he appeared alive at the mouth of the empty tomb is a mystery. Whatever the case, he was so changed by the experience that his best friends didn't even recognize him at first. (Sound familiar?) But the fact remains: He came back. He is alive. He conquered Satan, darkness, sin, and death once and for all.

Despite that fact, Satan hasn't surrendered. He's still waging battles and skirmishes. Like the Balrog on the bridge, he has decided, "If I must go down, then I will go down fighting. And I will do as much damage and bring as many people down with me as I can."

Think back to the first devotion. What battles or skirmishes are you witnessing—or fighting—right now? What can you do about them?

The answer is nothing—*on your own.*

Gandalf fought the battle and came back to help his friends win the war. Jesus fought the war and has come back to help us win our battles. We must surrender to his leadership rather than give in, skirmish by skirmish, to the onslaughts of darkness. Paul, writing a letter to the first Christians, says, "For you were once darkness, but now you are light in the Lord. Live as children of light" (Ephesians 5:8).

So what are you going to do about it?

You were once darkness, but now you are light in the Lord. Live as children of light.
EPHESIANS 5:8

THE WORD ON LIGHT

Take some time to read one or more of the following Bible passages:
2 Samuel 22:29; John 1:1-14; Ephesians 5:8-17; 1 Peter 2:9-12; 1 John 2:9-11

GOING FURTHER:

What was your reaction when you realized that Gandalf had come back?

As the Fellowship did with Gandalf, in what ways have you underestimated Jesus?

In what ways have you tried to fight the darkness on your own?

What does it mean to "live as children of light"?

What are you going to do about it?

WEEK TWO

CHOOSING
PRIDE
or
HUMILITY

Part One:

CHOOSING PRIDE

"Yet such is oft the course of deeds that move the wheels of the world: small hands do them because they must, while the eyes of the great are elsewhere."

—MASTER ELROND, FROM *THE FELLOWSHIP OF THE RING*, BOOK TWO, CHAPTER TWO

It's weird how you never really get a good look at the bad guy.

Except for that brief glimpse of the armor-clad Sauron in the opening moments of the first movie, there's no scene of the Dark Lord flexing his muscles and scaring the daylights out of everybody. You never see him on the throne of Mordor, barking out orders or plotting his next move. He is never shown pacing back and forth in the topmost part of the Dark Tower, muttering, "I must stop them. I *will* stop them!" In fact, the only thing you ever see is that enormous, unblinking Eye, rising above the fire and smoke to cast its awful gaze over Middle-earth.

The story goes that Sauron has no physical form. He lost it in the great battle at the end of the last age, when Isildur, one of Aragorn's ancestors, cut the Ring from his finger. He's been nothing but a Shadow ever since, a Being so dark and frightening that his own subjects can hardly stand to be in his presence. He's a character of great and terrible power, but his strength is not physical—it's psychological. He has convinced himself that he is something greater than he really is, and everyone else believes him.

He is pride itself.

Pride is the source of much of the tumult and conflict in *The Lord of the Rings:* the driving force behind the War of the Ring itself. It affects every character, from the greatest to the least, and no one is exempt from the struggle. Even the good guys, who want so desperately to save Middle-earth, face the temptation to think to themselves, *Perhaps I, alone of all, have the strength to accomplish this thing. Perhaps I could withstand the power of the Ring.* In short, they wish to fight strength with strength, pride with pride, insisting that their good motivations will exempt them from evil results.

Not so.

With his usual shrewdness, Tolkien puts a mirror in front of our faces, forcing us to look at our true selves.

If we're honest, pride is the primary motivation behind most of what we do—though our ambitions are nothing like Sauron's (thank goodness!). We instead pursue modest things like achievement, influence, comfort, security, and possessions—though when questioned closely about it, we're not likely to agree that's what we value most. We're more likely to express disgust at the self-centered values of others, insisting that *our* motivations are not only worthy but morally good. Or—and this is where it gets really sneaky—we publicly pretend to be horrified by our own failings, while inwardly believing ourselves to be far, far better than anyone else.

But this attitude is more insidious still. It's called *spiritual pride.*

Spiritual pride is when we're really, really glad that we're not like all those *other* people. It's when we've selflessly given up things that the world values in order to pursue what God wants, and it makes us feel, well . . . *better* than everyone else. We focus our energies on the spiritual activities that we find relatively enjoyable—going on mission trips, giving money, visiting old folks, going to church—and become blind to what God is really trying to accomplish through us in the world: a quiet revolution in which we put the needs of others before our own, no matter what the personal cost.

Jesus had the uncanny ability to expose the prideful motivations of others. He was especially exacting with the Pharisees, the religious leaders of his day, who felt that their "righteousness" made them superior to others. He knew that deep down they were pursuing the same worldly things as everyone else, though they pretended not to. This duplicity made him furious, and he said so. In fact, his denouncement of the Pharisees in Matthew 23 is enough to ruin for good any perception we might have that Jesus is just meek and mild.

Pride blinds us from seeing who we really are: small people with big problems who need help from Someone bigger still. It keeps us from seeing what God is really "up to" in the great battle between light and darkness. It causes us to miss out on the amazing things God is doing, beneath our very noses, through people we never even suspected. (Who would have guessed that the Ents of the forest of Fangorn would march to war? Or that a relatively unknown people from the Shire would save all of Middle-earth?)

If we're not careful, pride will undo us in the end. The famous proverb says, "Pride goes before destruction, a haughty spirit before a fall" (Proverbs 16:18). This is a painful truth for us personally, but for the good forces of Middle-earth, it is both their worst fear and their only hope.

As Gandalf well knows, pride has the potential to destroy the Fellowship, no matter how good everyone's motives may be. But pride may also be the key to Sauron's defeat. Gandalf explains this to Aragorn, Legolas, and Gimli: "That we should wish to cast him down and have *no* one in his place is not a thought that occurs to his mind. That we should try to destroy the Ring itself has not yet entered into his darkest dream."[8]

As Sauron's eye roves elsewhere, bent on securing his position of power, a small, frightened Hobbit named Frodo must make his way to the heart of darkness and cast the Ring into Mount Doom. It's a slim chance, but it just might work.

This is the lesson of Sauron from high in the Dark Tower of Mordor:

YOUR BIGGEST FOE IS PRIDE ITSELF.

So what are you going to do about it?

Pride goes before destruction, a haughty spirit before a fall.
PROVERBS 16:18

THE WORD ON PRIDE

Take some time to read one or more of the following Bible passages:
2 Samuel 22:28; Proverbs 11:2-3; Matthew 23:23-28; Luke 18:9-14

GOING FURTHER:

Why is pride so dangerous?

In what ways is pride perhaps blinding you from seeing yourself correctly?

Why did the Pharisees' attitude of spiritual pride make Jesus so angry (Matthew 23)?

In what ways have you seen spiritual pride at work in yourself or others?

What are you going to do about it?

Part Two:

CHOOSING HUMILITY

"And I suppose I must go alone, if I am to do that and save the Shire. But I feel very small, and very uprooted, and well—desperate. The Enemy is so strong and terrible."

—Frodo, from *The Fellowship of the Ring*, Book One,
Chapter Two

Frodo first sets out on his journey for the sake of the Shire. If his mission fails, the comfort and security of his homeland will be destroyed. But after a while he realizes that the Shire is only a small matter in the grand scheme of things. In fact, he may not be able to save it at all.

At that point he can give up the mission completely and tell the Council that someone else needs to take over. Or he can accept the job of Ring-bearer with a sense of puffed-up pride, thinking, *They trust me with this task? Then I must be someone pretty special. Think of the applause when I've accomplished it!* Or he can humble himself and do the task at hand—even if he sees no personal gain from it at all.

And that, of course, is what he does.

The word *humility* is related to *humus,* which means "dust" or "earth." In ancient times a humble person could be seen bowing at the feet of someone great, acknowledging that person's power and lordship. In that respect, the humble person was close to the ground—literally in the dust. This sounds degrading to us, but let's not forget where the word *human* comes from. God says to Adam in Genesis 3:19: "For dust you are and to dust you will return." God crafted Adam from the dust of the earth, and upon Adam's death that's what became of his body. We humans are no strangers to dust.

Yet there is a distinction between *humiliation* and *humility*. Humiliation is when someone *else* tells you to bow down—when someone else says, "You are dust." In that respect, Adam was clearly—and rightly—humiliated. This happens to all of us when we raise ourselves up too high, when we forget who we are.

Humility, on the other hand, is when we look upon the beloved face of one who is undoubtedly our Master and ask, "What must I do?"

Perhaps that's why a Hobbit is chosen for the task of Ring-bearer. The Hobbits are small folk, close to the ground. They do not fancy themselves as equals to the great and mighty people of Middle-earth. In fact, they want little to do with the glorious deeds of Men and Wizards and Elves. Consequently, the Ring does not have quite the same attraction and hold over these creatures as it does over the folks who think they are something special. Even though Bilbo, Frodo, and Sam are all vulnerable to the Ring's power, they fight it better than many others. Gandalf, who knows these dear Hobbits well, is prepared to stake everything on their innate humility.

Because Frodo is humble, he is willing to serve. He knows he doesn't have all of the answers. He isn't even sure that he'll accomplish the task. But he's willing, even though it breaks his heart to think of all that will be lost, knowing he might never, ever return to life as it was before he left the Shire. Little does he imagine the glorious outcome of his actions—the great celebration at "the end of all things," when Middle-earth is restored and the true King is enthroned in Gondor and the people rejoice in victory!

There is victory on the horizon for us as well—but

only if we're willing to humble ourselves and do whatever Jesus, our Master and King, puts before us.

Think of it this way: Say you're on an athletic team that faces a difficult foe. In order to win, there are several things that each player must do. First, the players must listen to the coach. This person has been put in charge for a reason: A good coach knows the game, knows his or her players' strengths and weaknesses, and knows what they're up against. If everyone does what the coach says, the team stands a better chance of winning. Second, the players must work together. If someone wants to show off and be a star without getting help from the rest, the whole team could lose.

Ironic, isn't it? It takes humility to win the game. It takes putting aside the desire to do things "your way" in order to do what your coach says. It takes putting aside your need for stardom in order to serve your teammates. This may seem tough at the time, but the adrenaline rush of victory—and the riotous fun afterward—make it all worth it in the end! After a win you hardly remember the rugged hard work of the game itself. Instead you tell story after story of the high points: "Remember that shot on goal? Remember that beautiful layup? Remember when they almost crushed our offense, and then so-and-so broke through and scored? Remember . . . ?" This is possible because you stood on the sidelines before the game and asked your coach, "What must I do?"

The apostle Peter wrote (from personal experience), "Humble yourselves, therefore, under God's mighty hand, that he may lift you up in due time" (1 Peter 5:6).

This is the lesson of Frodo, making his way into the heart of Sauron's kingdom:

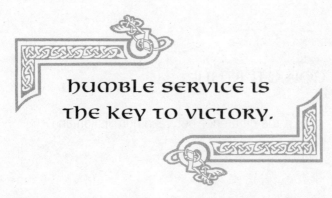

HUMBLE SERVICE IS THE KEY TO VICTORY.

So what are you going to do about it?

Humble yourselves, therefore, under God's mighty hand, that he may lift you up in due time.

1 PETER 5:6

THE WORD ON HUMILITY

Take some time to read one or more of the following Bible passages:

Psalm 45:4; Matthew 11:29-30; Ephesians 4:1-2; 1 Peter 5:5-6

GOING FURTHER:

What is the difference between humiliation and humility?

When have you experienced victory? What did it feel like?

How is Jesus like your coach?

In what specific areas of your life is he calling you to humbly serve others?

What are you going to do about it?

WEEK THREE

CHOOSING
CORRUPTION
or
INTEGRITY

Part One:

CHOOSING CORRUPTION

"True-hearted Men, they will not be corrupted. We of Minas Tirith have been staunch through long years of trial. We do not desire the power of the wizard-lords, only strength to defend ourselves, strength in a just cause."

—BOROMIR, FROM *THE FELLOWSHIP OF THE RING*, BOOK TWO, CHAPTER TEN

The word *corrupt* means, among other things, "decay." It's the same thing that happens to a sturdy house if it is not thoroughly inspected every once in a while. Water and moisture creep in behind the walls, rodents and insects gnaw away at the wood, and the foundation crumbles and fails to stand. If no one ever pokes around to see what might be rotting—and if decaying things are never replaced—the house will gradually fall to ruin.

Such is the case with the Stewards of Gondor. For many centuries they have ruled Gondor in the absence of any true heir to the throne, waiting for the day when they can usher the long-awaited king to his rightful seat. But in time they have come to enjoy the power of stewardship rather *too* much, a fact that is not hidden from the perceptive gaze of Gandalf. Believing themselves to be inherently sturdy in both body and soul, the current Steward, Denethor, and his eldest son, Boromir, are annoyed when others go poking around to test whether their motivations are really sound.

Of all the characters walking with Frodo, Boromir

never seems comfortable in the Council of the Wise. He is annoyed when Gandalf points out the weakness of Men in resisting the power of the Ring—and even more annoyed when the rest of the Fellowship echoes what Gandalf and Elrond have said. He is unwilling to be answerable to any of them, believing that the very worthiness of his cause is enough to justify his actions.

Boromir is a proud man, of a proud race of Men. In this he is much like his father. Lord Denethor has been keeping a great secret for years: He has one of the "seeing stones," the same kind that both Saruman and Sauron have in their possession. He believes that by sneaking a peek every now and then (in secret, of course), he can gain insight into the mind and plans of the Enemy. In his pride and arrogance, he believes that his good intentions will exempt him from evil consequences. He *is* strong enough to resist the Enemy, he insists, and is irritated if anyone suggests otherwise.

Thus, he and Gandalf are like oil and water; they can't seem to mix. By the time the wizard finally reaches the city of Minas Tirith in *The Return of the King*, Denethor wants nothing to do with him. He ignores Gandalf's probing questions and unbidden advice. He flinches at the very mention of accountability. Why should *he*, the Steward of Gondor, be answerable to a homeless wizard who—for all Denethor knows—might be in league with Sauron? Because Denethor's motives are corrupt, he sees everyone else's motives that way, too.

Denethor and Boromir react to Gandalf much like the person who believes his house to be solid: annoyed when someone suggests that the foundation might be unstable. If a homeowner is wise—and humble enough to admit there might be a problem—he will inspect the matter; he will admit that something is possibly wrong. But Boromir fails to do so until there are several dozen Orc arrows in his chest.

And his father never does at all.

To "take account" means to give an explanation. In financial terms, it means to double-check that the figures match the facts. That's the purpose of accounting firms in the world of business. People express surprise and disgust at the role these firms have played in corporate scandals throughout the years, but it makes sense, if you think about it. Suppose the person who is hired to inspect a building agrees to pretend that the building is sound—when it really isn't. The game lasts for a while, but then someone discovers that part of the structure is rotting. Upon probing further, they discover that the whole thing is a ruin because no one dared to address the signs of decay when they first appeared.

Without accountability, corruption is inevitable.

If this is true at the corporate level, it is also true at the spiritual level. "All a man's ways seem innocent to him," we read in the book of Proverbs, "but motives are weighed by the Lord" (16:2). One of the ways God tests our motives is through wise counselors—mentors, spiritual leaders, and teachers—who dare to "poke around" and inspect the soundness of our spiritual structure, looking for signs of decay. These are the Gandalfs and the Elronds of our lives. Without them, our good intentions can quickly disintegrate into bad actions that sabotage God's true purpose.

But this bothers us. We don't *want* people to inspect the soundness of our motives. We chafe at the very mention of accountability. We like to keep up the facade of righteousness (there's that spiritual pride again!) and go happily on our way, convinced that our good intentions will exempt us from evil consequences. And besides, it's no one else's business. Right?

Yet this is the lesson of Boromir and Denethor, the last in the line of Stewards of Gondor:

CORRUPTION COMES WHEN WE AVOID ACCOUNTABILITY.

So what are you going to do about it?

To the pure, all things are pure, but to those who are corrupted and do not believe, nothing is pure. In fact, both their minds and consciences are corrupted.
TITUS 1:15

THE WORD ON CORRUPTION

Take some time to read one or more of the following proverbs:
Proverbs 10:8-9, 17; 11:14; 14:11-12; 15:21-22; 16:2-3

GOING FURTHER:

What would you say are the driving motives behind your actions? Make a list.

In what ways have you failed to properly inspect the soundness of your motives?

What is your reaction when someone questions those motives?

What does that reaction show you about yourself?

What are you going to do about it?

Part Two:

CHOOSING INTEGRITY

Yet he felt in his heart that Faramir, though he was much like his brother in looks, was a man less self-regarding, both sterner and wiser.

—FROM *THE TWO TOWERS*, BOOK FOUR, CHAPTER FIVE

You show up for your first campus Bible-study meeting just a few minutes late and glance around the room. There's the expected crew of vocal Christians: the ones who lead prayer rallies and post flyers around school and preface every response in class with "Well, speaking as a Christian . . . " There's also the handful of kids you've never seen before: the quiet Christians. And then there's the surprise. Coleading the Bible study is someone you vaguely recognize. Where have you seen him before? Ah yes. The party Friday night.

Your reasons for being at the party were perfectly legitimate, of course. You did nothing that was not somehow defensible. But *this* guy . . . he was outrageous. And today he seems like a completely different person. In fact, he acts like he's never seen you before. So you play along. *All right,* you think. *Let's see how long he can keep up this game before he gets busted.*

This is similar to Samwise Gamgee's first suspicions of Boromir's brother, Faramir. (Sam is suspicious of everyone at first, until they prove faithful to his master, Frodo.) Faramir looks like his corrupted brother. He even acts like him, to some extent. The movie gives us every reason to doubt him. But, as Tolkien's readers know, Frodo discerns something about Faramir's character that is not perfectly obvious to Sam. It takes a test of Faramir's character for Sam to realize that the man has *integrity*. He is as different from his brother as day is from night.

When something has *integrity*, it is *integrated*. All the parts and pieces of it fit together to form a whole. That makes it structurally sound. When one or more of the pieces become corrupted or start to decay, the structure begins to *dis*-integrate. Unless the corrupted piece is removed or repaired, all the other pieces are eventually affected.

This is easy to see in the world of business. Every corporation is divided into departments. Each department has its own role and function, yet each is responsible to the others for performing its assigned tasks. When all the departments share the same mission and the same goals, the corporation holds together. It is integrated. It has integrity. But when one department has a different mission from the others—or fails to communicate its activities to the others—the corporation begins to fall apart. It is no longer integrated. It no longer has integrity.

That's what happens when corrupt corporations get caught in financial scandals. Most of the employees had no idea that anything illegal was going on. If they had, the illegal activities wouldn't have continued for very long without someone quitting and blowing the whistle (in fact, that's how most of the companies get caught).

A lot of us divide life into departments, too: the Home Department, the School Department, the Work Department, the Church Department, the Friends Department, etc. It's a defense mechanism against chaos, allowing us to tackle one thing at a time without getting overwhelmed. The problem comes when we begin to have different motives and behaviors from one department to another. It's like we become several different people instead of one person. We are no longer integrated. We no longer have integrity.

WALKING WITH FRODO 🔲 55

Imagine what it feels like to be an employee of a corporation caught in financial scandal. You had no idea that anything wrong was happening. You feel hurt and betrayed and even disgusted. It's the same reaction you might have to the coleader of your Bible study—or to any "strong" Christian who acts differently from setting to setting. And it's the same reaction others have toward *you,* when you say one thing but do another.

So what makes Faramir different from his brother and father? Not only is he a man of integrity whose various life "departments" are integrated to form a whole, but he also is willing to be held accountable. He is the only one in his family who listens to Gandalf when Gandalf probes to see what might not be holding together. Faramir knows his own limitations. He realizes that he could easily be corrupted, easily become *dis*-integrated. With humility, he allows Gandalf to hold him accountable. And he ultimately proves faithful.

The psalmist asks, "How can a young man keep his way pure? By living according to your word. I seek you with all my heart; do not let me stray from your commands" (Psalm 119:9-10). In the effort to keep our lives integrated, free of corruption, we can't go it alone. We need God's strength and counsel. We must seek out and heed the wisdom God brings us through the Gandalfs in our lives.

This is the lesson of Faramir, faced with the temptation of the Ring at Henneth Annûn:

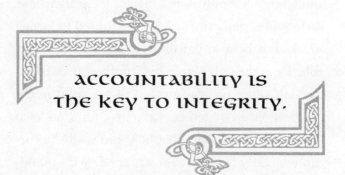

ACCOUNTABILITY IS
THE KEY TO INTEGRITY.

So what are you going to do about it?

He who listens to a life-giving rebuke will be at home among the wise. He who ignores discipline despises

himself, but whoever heeds correction gains under-
standing.
Proverbs 15:31-32

THE WORD ON INTEGRITY

Take some time to read one or more of the following Bible passages:
2 Samuel 22:26-27; Psalm 15; 119:9-10; Proverbs
16:20; 22:11; Daniel 6:4; Ephesians 4:22-24;
1 Peter 1:22-23

GOING FURTHER:

Make a list of your life "departments" (school,
family, friends, church, etc.).

How well are the "departments" of your life
integrated?

What message does that send to others about your true character?

Who can keep you accountable to staying integrated?

What are you going to do about it?

WEEK
FOUR

CHOOSING
BETRAYAL
or
LOYALTY

Part One:

CHOOSING BETRAYAL

"We'll be nice to them, very nice, if they'll be nice to us, won't we, yes, yes."
—GOLLUM, FROM *THE TWO TOWERS*, BOOK FOUR, CHAPTER ONE

Walking with Frodo on the crooked road to Mordor is one of the most memorable characters in all literature.

Gollum.

When he first appears on the big screen, live and in color, the CGI geeks lean forward, drooling, while the rest of us shrink back in our seats with a mixture of horror and fascination. So it is when we read the books. He is the personification of slime: slippery with decay, inside and out.

The character of Gollum is so corrupted and *dis*-integrated that his separate personalities actually have conversations with each other. He speaks in the plural: "we" wishes this and "we" wants that. One personality seems to be loyal to Frodo; the other hopes to kill him at the soonest opportunity. But both have this in common: Gollum is primarily concerned about what's best for Gollum. He will be faithful to his master *only if* it accomplishes his true purpose: to recapture the Ring for himself.

The relationship is built on conditions. *If* the Hobbits are nice to him, Gollum will be nice, too. *If* the "fat Hobbit" (Samwise, of course) treats him with some measure of respect, Gollum will lead

Master Frodo where he needs to go. But at the merest hint that Frodo or Sam is being "tricksy" or "false," Gollum starts scheming about how to get back at him—and the whole dangerous game begins again.

It's like walking on ice. Those of you who have ever done so know how creepy it is the first few times. The ice appears thick and secure; it looks like it will hold. But you've heard far too many stories about people who have fallen through. So you place each foot carefully, wondering if the next will be your last. If the ice holds, you gradually begin to gain confidence that it will continue to do so. But if there's even the merest hint of instability, you retreat as fast as you can.

The scary part is that you can't always tell the difference between ice that is treacherous and ice that is solid. It depends on the conditions. *If* the weather has been cold enough and the sun hasn't been too hot and the weight you're carrying isn't too great, *then* the ice will hold. But you fear becoming too confident because you never know when that which looks solid will actually prove too thin to support you.

So it is with many of our friendships. A person may appear solid and loyal on the outside, but the veneer of fidelity may be only an inch thick. Or the relationship may actually be quite strong—but only under certain conditions. And sometimes you don't realize that you've been betrayed until your foot slips and down you go.

The person who lacks integrity—whose various life "departments" are not integrated—has divided loyalties. In one "department" she is loyal to herself; in another, she is loyal to her best friend, or to God, her parents, her studies, and so on. Depending on the context or the situation, she is the most faithful friend or daughter or Christian you could ever hope to meet. But encounter her in a different context, when her loyalty is placed elsewhere, and the things she says or does will take you completely by surprise.

Jesus knows what it feels like to be on the receiving end of such behavior. Not only did his friend Judas, who walked with him for years, betray him to the chief priests for a lousy bribe of thirty pieces of silver, but Peter, that stalwart, trusty disciple (whose name, ironically, means "rock"), denied even knowing him at all. In the "Faithful Disciple" Department, Peter was quick to claim, "Lord, I am ready to go with you to prison and to death" (Luke 22:33). But just a few hours later, in the "Saving My Reputation" Department, Peter was a completely different person. The conditions had changed. It was no longer cool (or safe) to walk with Jesus.

In this we all stand indicted. We are both sinned against and sinning. We love our friends "on condition" (*if* they're nice to us, *if* they stand up for us, *if, if, if*...). And we treat God the same way: "I'll do this for God *if* he'll do that for me," or "I'll stand up for God *if* he lets me look cool at the same time," or "I'll sacrifice this thing *if* God will give me that other thing." But what if God doesn't pull through on any of the conditions we place on him? Will we, like Gollum, call our Master "tricksy" and "false" and play "false" ourselves? Or will we trust that our Master has a plan, and stick by him no matter what?

This is the lesson of Gollum, who leads Frodo and Sam ever closer to Mordor:

THE RELATIONSHIP BUILT ON CONDITIONS WILL ULTIMATELY BETRAY YOU.

So what are you going to do about it?

No one can serve two masters. Either he will hate the one and love the other, or he will be devoted to the one and despise the other.
MATTHEW 6:24

THE WORD ON BETRAYAL

Take some time to read one or more of the following Bible passages:
1 Samuel 12:20-22; Psalm 25:1-3; Isaiah 59:12-13; Jeremiah 3:19-20; Matthew 26:14-16; 27:1-5

GOING FURTHER:

When have you felt betrayed by a friend?

What did it feel like?

How did you respond?

Review your list of life "departments" from last time. In which departments are you loyal to God? In which are you loyal to something else?

What are you going to do about it?

Part Two:

choosing loyalty

Now they were come to the bitter end. But he had stuck to his master all the way; that was what he had chiefly come for, and he would still stick to him. His master would not go to Mordor alone.

—From *The Two Towers*, Book Four, Chapter Three

Where *would* Frodo be without Sam?

He "wouldn't have got far," that's for sure. Not only does Sam save his friend and master, time and time again, but also he could easily be credited with saving all of Middle-earth, though he'd be painfully embarrassed to think so.

That's because Sam doesn't think of Sam at all. He doesn't break his life down into separate "departments," serving his own needs in one area and his friend's needs in another. He has one purpose—to stick by his master—and that purpose carries him from circumstance to circumstance, never wavering, never faltering, never giving up. If he ends up a hero in the end, great—it will be a nice story to tell later. But if he doesn't, that's fine, too. As long as he fulfills his promise to remain close, he is content with whatever life brings.

It's a curious thing, really. We think of him fondly as a rather simple, uncomplicated soul, as if the choice to stick by Frodo would have been easier for him than it would be for us. But is that really true? Sam constantly debates himself over whether or not to trust "Stinker" and "Slinker" (his names for the split personalities of Gollum). He argues with himself over what to do after Shelob attacks Frodo and there is no one to take the Ring on to Mount Doom. Should he leave his master, cold and—to all appearances—dead on the trail, and fulfill the task of destroying the Ring, or should he stick by his master, though it will mean the failure of the mission? Not long after he makes his choice, he knows he chose wrong, and he frantically backtracks to try and make it right again.

No, the decisions are not easy for Sam. Even he feels the temptation of the Ring for the brief time in which he carries it. He wrestles to discern what is the right road, the most loyal choice. He struggles to blend the various "departments" of his life into one unified whole in which his master's needs come first. But he does it one step at a time. He talks himself through it, he thinks out loud, he argues back and forth—not unlike Gollum, for that matter—until he finally pulls through.

And we can do the same.

We've heard it many times. We can practically quote by heart Jesus' words: "If anyone would come after me, he must deny himself and take up his cross and follow me. For whoever wants to save his life will lose it, but whoever loses his life for me will find it" (Matthew 16:24-25). He's talking about unconditional love. But love without conditions does not come easily to us. We want to know, "What's in it for me?" We weigh the risks first, and if it looks like we'll lose more than we can stand to give, we back away.

And besides that, our loyalties are often so scattered among our various life "departments" that the thought of aligning them all under one Master can be exhausting. It takes tremendous time and energy to make Jesus Lord of our homes, families, classes, work, and friendships. But the call is there. Either we walk with Jesus in every aspect of our lives, or we don't walk with him at all.

St. John of the Cross, a sixteenth-century monk,

said that we are willing to sacrifice only insofar as it makes us feel good. As long as going on mission trips and giving money and visiting old folks and going to church is relatively painless, we're willing to stick it out. But when the going gets tough, the tough wimp out completely. As G. K. Chesterton wrote, "The Christian ideal has not been tried and found wanting; it has been found difficult and left untried." [9]

The test of our character is whether or not we'll stick it out with Jesus when there no longer appears to be anything in it for us personally. Will we keep walking with Jesus when our friends no longer think it's cool? Will we stick it out when the leaders of our mission trip are fighting? when we really can't afford to tithe? when the old folks get snippy or take our visits for granted? when our church's worship service bores us to tears?

The single-hearted devotion of Sam is an ever-elusive goal in our spiritual lives. Yet here's the beauty of serving Jesus: When we mess up, when our loyalties are conflicted, when we make disloyal choices, there is grace to make everything right again. We have not lost our last and best chance to prove our faithfulness. We are given the wisdom and the power and the undivided heart to get up and try again. And when we do, what stories will be told about our lives!

This is the lesson of Samwise Gamgee, walking with his master, Frodo, to the very end:

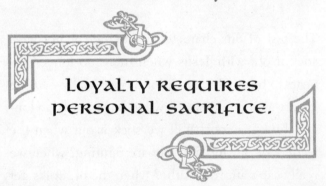

LOYALTY REQUIRES PERSONAL SACRIFICE.

So what are you going to do about it?

Teach me your way, O Lord, and I will walk in your truth; give me an undivided heart, that I may fear your name.
PSALM 86:11

THE WORD ON LOYALTY

Take some time to read one or more of the following Bible passages:
1 Chronicles 29:17-19; Proverbs 18:24;
Ecclesiastes 4:9-12; John 15:13

GOING FURTHER:

When have you found it difficult to be loyal to Jesus?

What sacrifices are you being asked to make in order to "stick it out" with Jesus?

How does it feel, knowing there is grace when you "mess up"?

What tales will be told about you, when it's all said and done?

What are you going to do about it?

WEEK FIVE

CHOOSING
DISUNITY
or
FORGIVENESS

Part One:

CHOOSING DISUNITY

*"If this nice friendliness would spread about in Mordor,
half our trouble would be over."*

—SAM TO FRODO, FROM *THE RETURN OF THE KING*, BOOK SIX,
CHAPTER TWO

All is not well in the land of Mordor—good news for the good forces of Middle-earth. But the danger remains.

Each unit of Orcs is rather like a body part, keeping the whole thing running. When each *unit* is doing its job, the whole body has *unity*, and the hosts of Mordor are *unified.* But festering beneath the surface are resentments and betrayals—the result of wounded pride. The units occasionally break out and fight each other. And nothing threatens Sauron's schemes more than disunity and disintegration among his troops.

So how does he prevent this from happening? By making his subjects so terrified of him that they dare not disobey. They overlook their disagreements only because they fear Sauron more than they care about their wounded pride. But the minute they find the slightest excuse to destroy each other, they do so without even a hint of remorse. Their appearance of unity is only pretense. Deep down, it's "every Orc for himself."

Merry and Pippin see this firsthand during their dreadful kidnapping in *The Two Towers*. There appear to be two units of Orc creatures among their kidnappers: the Northerners from Mordor, instructed to bring the Hobbits to Sauron; and the Uruk-hai of Isengard, with their secret mission to bring the Hobbits to Saruman instead. It doesn't take long before the two units are at each other's throats.

Frodo and Sam find much the same situation once they cross the border into Mordor. Everywhere they turn, it seems, Orcs are doing half the work by killing each other in one betrayal after another. But the Hobbits dare not forget that the Orcs are still unified by their fear of Sauron and a desire to save their own skins. After a close encounter with two fighting Orcs, Frodo tells Sam, "If those two had seen us, they would have dropped all their quarrel until we were dead."[10]

Sauron knows that disunity is at work among his enemies (though he ignores it in his own troops).

He is counting on the natural selfishness of each kingdom to gradually bring about the disintegration of the hosts that rise against him. If all goes well, in his estimation, half the battle will be over before his hosts ever cross the border into Gondor.

You've seen this principle yourself. Perhaps you've experienced it in your family. Or maybe you've watched it happen within your church or youth group. Everyone seems happy and smiling and together on the outside, but deep down there are wounded relationships and little betrayals, breaking apart the Christian community from the inside out.

Jesus said, "Every kingdom divided against itself will be ruined, and every city or household divided against itself will not stand" (Matthew 12:25). Any sense of unity created by self-interest will not last. This is one of the spiritual laws of the universe. A marriage begins to break apart when the partners no longer serve each other but rather themselves. Their pride is easily wounded. They allow resentments and feelings of bitterness to fester until the whole relationship explodes at once, destroying the household.

The same thing can happen with a church or Christian group. The members pretend to focus on the mission when, in fact, they have their own personal agendas in mind. The moment their personal agendas are threatened, they become defensive and angry. They begin to harbor resentments, allowing bitterness to bubble beneath the surface until the whole pot boils over.

We all have Orc-like tendencies when forced to live and work together with others. This is especially true within families and churches, where we don't get to choose our companions. There is tremendous pressure to pretend we like each other, while at the same time avoiding the healthy kind of communication that might successfully hold the unit together.

The evil one is well aware of this principle, though he tries to ignore it in his own kingdom. Instead, he focuses on bringing about division within the kingdom of God—particularly in the sacred places of home and church. He takes particular pleasure in creating little rumblings of discord, then sitting back to watch the relationships erupt on their own.

This is the lesson of the Orcs, forced to work together and accomplish the will of Sauron:

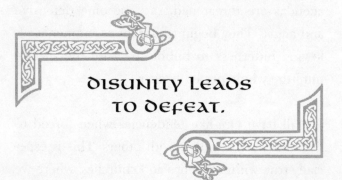

DISUNITY LEADS TO DEFEAT.

So what are you going to do about it?

An angry man stirs up dissension, and a hot-tempered one commits many sins.
PROVERBS 29:22

THE WORD ON DISUNITY

Take some time to read one or more of the following Bible passages:
Proverbs 6:12-14, 16-19; 16:28; Romans 13:13-14; Galatians 5:19-21

GOING FURTHER:

Where have you seen disunity in your home or church?

What is (or was) the result?

How has it affected you personally, particularly in your attitude toward church or family?

How have you let your wounded pride or personal ambitions stand in the way of getting along with others?

What are you going to do about it?

Part Two:

CHOOSING FORGIVENESS

"Indeed in nothing is the power of the Dark Lord more clearly shown than in the estrangement that divides all those who still oppose him."

—HALDIR, FROM *THE FELLOWSHIP OF THE RING*, BOOK TWO, CHAPTER SIX

If it weren't for the "comic relief" of Gimli and Legolas (and Merry and Pippin and the Ents), *The Lord of the Rings* would be a very dark tale indeed. We need to laugh out loud *sometimes,* as Tolkien well knew, or therapists might be up in arms about the epidemic of *LOTR*-Induced Depressive Disorder.

So we laugh at Gimli and Legolas and their fun-loving competitiveness. But there's something important to keep in mind: The history of the strained relationship between Dwarves and Elves is no laughing matter.

These two races have had a long-standing feud spanning hundreds of years. The "record of wrongs" is lengthy on both sides, including betrayal, murder, imprisonment, and outright war. The Elves and Dwarves even manage to drag this "record of wrongs" into the Council of Elrond, prompting sharp debate that threatens to tear the Council at the seams. Gandalf is right to intercede before things fall apart, saying, "If all the grievances that stand between Elves and Dwarves are to be brought up here, we may as well abandon this Council."[11]

Without unity, the Fellowship is doomed to failure. And the only way to achieve unity is if the Elves and Dwarves dare to forgive one another.

We are called to do the same—though the discussion is not just about racial reconciliation and political correctness and all the nice, sappy stuff that's been shoved at us since kindergarten. It's about examining *every single one* of our relationships—particularly in the context of family and church.

The apostle Paul says that love "keeps no record of wrongs" (1 Corinthians 13:5). If you truly love a person, you don't keep a mental list of all the ways he or she has hurt you. You don't add up all the ways a sibling has put you down or a friend has betrayed you or a parent has failed to trust you. When you do, it's far too tempting to drag the list out in the heat of an argument and go through it point by point, like a lawyer making a case.

Most of the time, however, you may not even be aware that you're keeping a list. It's sort of like a pot of water on the burner of a gas stove. The first time a person hurts you, the flame is lit. The next time he or she hurts you, the flame goes up a notch. The third time, the flame goes up some more. Soon the water is beginning to bubble. Then, without warning, your emotional pot boils over and you lash out at the person. He or she walks away thinking, *What was that about? All I said was "good morning"!*

We've already discussed how such things delight the enemy—particularly in the context of the Christian community. Christ's followers wrestled with it from the beginning. Peter asked Jesus, "Lord, how many times shall I forgive my brother when he sins against me? Up to seven times?" Jesus answered, "I tell you, not seven times, but seventy-seven times" (Matthew 18:21-22). In other words, stop keeping a list. Turn off the burner. Forgive your Christian sisters and brothers without dragging in all the ways they failed you before and all the ways they'll probably fail you again. Don't fall into the enemy's trap.

For the Fellowship, it's a matter of life or death. Even as they set forth, Legolas and Gimli are throwing verbal darts at each other, with Gandalf as referee. Then just as they begin to reach some semblance of unity, the Fellowship loses Gandalf in the Mines of Moria and flees to Lothlórien. There, according to the book, the Elves insist that the Dwarf must be blindfolded if he is to enter the realm of Galadriel without being killed on the spot. Things almost come to blows before Aragorn wisely suggests that they *all* be blindfolded.

It isn't until Gimli meets the lady Galadriel herself that the healing is complete: "And the Dwarf . . . looked up and met her eyes; and it seemed to him that he looked suddenly into the heart of an enemy and saw there love and understanding."[12]

From that point on, Gimli and Legolas are inseparable. They are still competitors, in a fun-loving way, but each knows full well that the other would gladly die for him. The long record of wrongs on both sides of the conflict is forgiven, erased. And the Dark Lord of Mordor learns the hard way that such a friendship, such a Fellowship, is a threat to his very existence.

This is the lesson of Legolas and Gimli, sworn to eternal friendship:

FORGIVENESS IS YOUR STRONGEST DEFENSE AGAINST THE ENEMY.

So what are you going to do about it?

Bear with each other and forgive whatever grievances you may have against one another. Forgive as the Lord forgave you.
COLOSSIANS 3:13

THE WORD ON FORGIVENESS

Take some time to read one or more of the following Bible passages:
Psalm 133:1; Matthew 6:12-15; Luke 6:37-38;
Romans 15:5; 2 Corinthians 2:5-8; Philippians
2:1-2; Colossians 3:13-15

GOING FURTHER:

In what ways have you kept a record of wrongs against someone else?

In what ways have others kept a record of wrongs against you?

If people in your family or church were to erase their record of wrongs against each other, what would change?

What does it take to express and experience forgiveness?

What are you going to do about it?

WEEK
SIX

CHOOSING
DECEIT
or
HONESTY

Part One:

CHOOSING DECEIT

"And ever Wormtongue's whispering was in your ears, poisoning your thought, chilling your heart, weakening your limbs, while others watched and could do nothing, for your will was in his keeping."

—GANDALF TO KING THÉODEN, FROM *THE TWO TOWERS*, BOOK THREE, CHAPTER SIX

If the enemy can't have you on his side, he'll make sure you're no good to the other. But he doesn't dare attack you openly in case it might rouse you to take some meaningful action against him. So instead he pushes you by slow, calculated degrees toward the darkness. Working from the angle of truth, he gradually distorts it, bit by bit, until you believe nothing but lies. He uses slow poison to weaken your spirit until you are no longer a threat to his kingdom.

Such is the case with Wormtongue.

The argument could be made that he truly loved King Théoden—once; that he really did have Rohan's best interests in mind—at one time. Yet somehow during the course of service to the king he has come under the influence of the wizard Saruman, who himself was once loyal to the cause of good in Middle-earth. Perhaps that's what deceived Wormtongue into believing Saruman in the first place. By degrees Wormtongue has come under Saruman's influence, and through Wormtongue, Théoden has as well—without even being aware of it.

The king is old, after all. He has suffered some tremendous personal blows, such as the loss of his son the prince and the absence of any help from the land of Gondor. At first, Wormtongue's suggestions are perhaps wise—take it easy, don't move too quickly, use caution to discern if this evil is really as bad as it looks. Find out who your true friends are before you trust anyone too quickly. But in time, Wormtongue begins to worry about Wormtongue more than he worries about the king. His suggestions, though veiled as loyalty to his master, are actually more about saving his own skin and securing his own position of power.

While we don't know the whole story of what brought Wormtongue to this point, we can make some educated guesses. Somewhere along the way, Wormtongue becomes aware of a powerful force rising in Middle-earth—a force against which it would not be wise to fight if one values one's life and safety. If his king were to become cognizant of the situation and choose to act upon it, Wormtongue would risk having to go to war by the king's side. It might mean a great deal of personal suffering—something Wormtongue would rather avoid at all costs. So he begins to weave a web of deception that will hold Théoden in place, that will render him helpless, that will secure Wormtongue's position of comfort and influence. And in time, not only does Théoden believe him, but Wormtongue believes himself.

We all have something in our lives that we would rather not face. Usually it's some aspect of obedience in the fight against evil, something that requires a great deal of personal sacrifice, or suffering, or humility. Perhaps it's confessing something to our parents that we'd rather they didn't know, or kicking an addiction, or apologizing to a friend, or acknowledging some secret sin to one of our spiritual mentors. Our fear of the consequences becomes so powerful that we begin to invent reasons why we should not have to face them. Pretty soon we believe those reasons are real—and we try to convince others they are too.

Often, however, we only mildly mishandle the truth, twisting it now and then to put ourselves in a better light, or to flatter someone else to get them to do what we want. The psalmist says, "Everyone lies to his neighbor; their flattering lips speak with deception" (Psalm 12:2), and Paul reiterates that "such people are not serving our Lord Christ, but their own appetites. By smooth talk and flattery they deceive the minds of naive people" (Romans 16:18). The game is as old as the Garden of Eden, but the consequences are the same.

What we fail to realize is that when we tell a lie, we are bound to that lie until the people who know the truth (namely ourselves) have forgotten it or until the lie is confessed. Before long we have created an intricate system of lies to support the original one, which together produce an epic myth that takes every ounce of energy to sustain. The truth becomes a minefield through which we have to

walk so carefully that we can hardly enjoy what
we're doing or where we're going. Things are far
worse than if we had dared to face the consequences of telling the truth in the first place.

Wormtongue learns this lesson the hard way. As
the cinematic version shows, he doesn't even know
the extent of what he has done until he stands on
the battlement of Orthanc at Saruman's side, sur-
veying the host of Uruk-hai before the attack on
Rohan, one lone tear trickling down his cheek.

This is the lesson of Wormtongue as reality finally
sinks in:

THE TRUTH IS NEVER
SO HARMFUL AS THE
CONSEQUENCES
OF DECEIT.

So what are you going to do about it?

In fact, everyone who wants to live a godly life in Christ Jesus will be persecuted, while evil men and impostors will go from bad to worse, deceiving and being deceived.
2 TIMOTHY 3:12-13

THE WORD ON DECEIT

Take some time to read one or more of the following Bible passages:
Isaiah 59:12-15; Jeremiah 7:3-8; Luke 16:10;
John 8:43-47; Romans 16:17-18; Ephesians
5:6-7; 1 John 1:8-10

GOING FURTHER:

Make a list of things you know God is calling you to do—things that you would rather avoid. What future tasks would you rather not face?

In what ways have you tried to convince yourself
(and others) that you don't have to face those
things?

Based on Wormtongue's experience, what are the
consequences of self-deception? of deceiving
others?

What are you going to do about it?

Part Two:

CHOOSING HONESTY

"I owe much to Éomer," said Théoden. "Faithful heart may have forward tongue."

—FROM *THE TWO TOWERS,* BOOK THREE, CHAPTER SIX

Picture this: Three good friends are sharing a dorm room. They're the kind of friends who will stand up in one another's weddings someday. One afternoon while two of them are hanging out in the room, they accidentally discover a bag of weed in the third roommate's jacket pocket. Time stops for a moment. They grow silent, trying to decide what to do. Finally the discussion begins, one halting sentence at a time. They will do something, and they will do it now. One of them makes a phone call. The other paces around the room, jiggling his car keys. Then they sit and wait.

When their friend walks in the door an hour later, they talk him into going with them for a Slurpee. Then the moment the car is out of the parking lot, the truth comes out.

"We found the weed."

"We don't know if you've even been using it, or for how long. . . ."

"But that's not the point. The point is that we care about you, man. We're going to a counselor."

"And before you get really mad, we need to tell you something else. If either of us saw you standing in the path of a speeding truck, we would throw ourselves in the way. So you'd better believe we will do whatever it takes to keep you from getting hurt."

Imagine what it would feel like to be the friend they confronted. What would be your gut reaction? What conflicting emotions would go on inside of you? How would it feel to have those friends "invade" your privacy and put their nose in "your business"? How would it feel to hear something put so bluntly, so honestly?

Now imagine what it would feel like to be one of the roommates. What would your gut reaction be when you found out what your friend was doing? How would it feel to know you would have to confront someone about behavior that was possibly destructive? What would your love for your roommate compel you to do?

Welcome to Éomer's world.

He is painfully aware that his uncle, King Théoden, is sinking further and further into decrepitude. Somehow the counselor Wormtongue has made himself the king's right-hand man. Théoden now says and does the wimpiest, most *un*kingly things, rendered nearly powerless by the web of deception he has allowed Wormtongue to weave around him. Éomer wants nothing more than to confront the king with the truth, to fling wide the dark curtains that have fallen over his soul, and to let the light come streaming in.

All of us have had friends or family members like Théoden. We watch them sink by slow degrees into a false world of their own making. Perhaps they have an addiction that they'd rather not kick. Maybe they're just spiritually numb. Or maybe they're in outright rebellion against the Light. Whatever it is, they create their own reality and then buttress it with whatever excuses or arguments or lies they can manufacture. Because they are afraid someone will attempt to point out the truth, they cut themselves off from friends, from family, from faith or church or whatever has kept them anchored. We watch them drift away, though we want nothing more than to swim after them and haul them back in. But out of fear that we'll push them even further away, we say and do nothing.

Éomer, by contrast, takes action. While Tolkien doesn't discuss all that has taken place in the court of the king prior to the arrival of Gandalf, Aragorn, Legolas, and Gimli, we get the impression that Éomer has spoken his mind at times, exposing the truth whether the king will listen or not. If he is mistaken for being faithless, so be it. He knows that he is faithful. His love for the king is what compels him to speak the truth. And if he suffers for it—if he loses the king's favor or is imprisoned or banished or worse—in the long run it is a small price to pay for saving the king's soul.

So why is that *so hard* to do in real life?

In this battle we fight against the prevailing winds

of culture. The statement "It's none of your business" just about sums it up. And none of us are exempt from that attitude. Having been steeped in the cultural value of autonomy for so long, we're not even aware of how much it has a hold on us—until someone dares to confront us about our behavior (or until we crash and burn). Then reality sets in. Our actions *are* destructive. They *do* affect others. We *have* been living a lie.

The apostle James put it bluntly: "My brothers, if one of you should wander from the truth and someone should bring him back, remember this: Whoever turns a sinner from the error of his way will save him from death and cover over a multitude of sins" (James 5:19-20).

This is the lesson of Éomer, choosing to be honest with King Théoden:

LOVE DARES TO SPEAK THE TRUTH, NO MATTER WHAT THE COST.

So what are you going to do about it?

My brothers, if one of you should wander from the truth and someone should bring him back, remember this: Whoever turns a sinner from the error of his way will save him from death and cover over a multitude of sins.

JAMES 5:19-20

THE WORD ON HONESTY

Take some time to read one or more of the following Bible passages:

Psalm 51:3-6; Proverbs 12:17-22; 1 Corinthians
13:6; Ephesians 4:14-16; 6:14; Colossians 3:9-10

GOING FURTHER:

When has someone dared to be honest with you?

What was the outcome of his or her decision to
speak up?

Whom do you need to confront with the truth?
Why?

What is holding you back?

What are you going to do about it?

WEEK
SEVEN

CHOOSING
BONDAGE
or
FREEDOM

Part One:

CHOOSING BONDAGE

"Now, lord," said Gandalf, *"look out upon your land!*
Breathe the free air again!"
—GANDALF TO KING THÉODEN, FROM *THE TWO TOWERS*, BOOK
THREE, CHAPTER SIX

King Théoden has been rendered powerless. Perhaps it's Wormtongue's fault. Perhaps it's Saru-

man's. Perhaps the king's loyal subjects should have joined with Éomer in honest, "froward" speech that might have possibly saved their lord from the slow journey into decay. All of these certainly contributed to the problem. But when the king finally comes to his senses, he rightly perceives that he has no one to blame but himself. He alone, upon glimpsing the dark, uncertain future, made the choice to hide from it in fear.

Fear drives us to do strange things—or to do nothing at all. Fear of the truth makes us tell half-truths, which lead to lies, which lead to a life that *is* a lie. Fear of rejection or betrayal makes us avoid being vulnerable with others, till we lose all sense of need for human companionship. Fear of loneliness makes us cling to others with such exhausting tenacity that we never have a moment for self-reflection to remember who we really are. Fear of failure paralyzes us until we are no longer able to act in meaningful ways.

What we fail to realize is that the moment we act out of fear, that fear has mastery over us. Take failure, for example. Sure, we know the mantra "If at first you don't succeed, try and try again." But most of the time we approach life's challenges more like Homer Simpson: "Trying is the first step toward failure." ("D'oh!") So why try? If we don't do anything, we can't be responsible for what happens, right? With that attitude, we have successfully rendered ourselves powerless to impact the future in a meaningful way. We've jumped into a self-imposed cage and locked the door. And contrary to what we like to tell ourselves, failing to act is just as sinful as actively rebelling against God.

Jesus told a parable along those lines in Matthew 25:14-30. A powerful lord goes away on a long journey. Before he leaves, he gives to each of three servants a sum of money to invest. The first two servants invest well—the money makes more money. But the third servant, knowing his lord is a hard taskmaster, fearfully buries the money until the lord comes back. His master is furious. Sure, the servant could have invested the money and lost it all, but that would have been more impressive than doing nothing. His master says to "throw that worthless servant outside, into the darkness, where there will be weeping and gnashing of teeth" (Matthew 25:30). The servant's failure to act led to more bondage than if he had acted and failed.

History has proven the truth of that story. World War II, for example, was a dark time, when the right way did not always seem clear to peace-loving people. Even when leaders like Winston Churchill eloquently defended the call to meaningful action, people were often reluctant to do anything in response. Some Christians, however, acted openly against the darkness. Among them was Dietrich Bonhoeffer, a pastor who was executed by the Nazis for allegedly plotting to assassinate Hitler. Bonhoeffer wrote, "Mere waiting and looking on is not Christian behavior. The Christian is called to sympathy and to action."[13] Had Bonhoeffer not acted, he would have thrown himself into a spiritual prison far more demoralizing than anything the Nazis could have done to him.

The moment we face our fears honestly and bravely, the lock on our self-imposed cage is de-

stroyed and the door flings wide open to freedom.
The moment Théoden finally wakes up, he turns
to Gandalf and asks, "What is your counsel?"
Gandalf replies, "You have yourself already taken
it. . . . To put your trust in Éomer, rather than in a
man of crooked mind. To cast aside regret and
fear. To do the deed at hand."[14]

This is the lesson of Théoden, facing a future of
dark uncertainty:

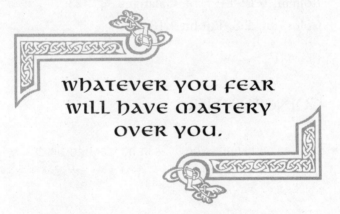

WHATEVER YOU FEAR
WILL HAVE MASTERY
OVER YOU.

So what are you going to do about it?

*Don't you know that when you offer yourselves to
someone to obey him as slaves, you are slaves to the one*

whom you obey—whether you are slaves to sin, which leads to death, or to obedience, which leads to righteousness?
ROMANS 6:16

THE WORD ON BONDAGE

Take some time to read one or more of the following Bible passages:
Psalm 107:10-16; Proverbs 29:25; Acts 8:22-23; Romans 6:12-14; 7:14; Galatians 3:22-23; Colossians 2:8; 1 John 4:18

GOING FURTHER:

Who do you know who lives in bondage to sin or fear?

How does that affect his or her ability to act in meaningful ways?

Make a list of your own worst fears. What is at the root of each of them?

In what ways have you become bound to those fears? In other words, in what ways do they have mastery over you?

What are you going to do about it?

Part Two:

CHOOSING FREEDOM

"What do you fear, lady?" he asked.

"A cage," she said. *"To stay behind bars, until use and old age accept them, and all chance of doing great deeds is gone beyond recall or desire."*

—ARAGORN AND ÉOWYN, FROM *THE RETURN OF THE KING*, BOOK FIVE, CHAPTER TWO

John Calvin, the sixteenth-century Protestant leader, said that most people "fear and abhor" three things: poverty, obscurity, and humility.

Why those three? What do they have in common? Well, all involve sacrifice: in poverty, giving up the need to have the stuff we want; in obscurity, giving up the need to make a name for ourselves; and in humility, giving up the need to pursue *our* personal agendas first.

But perhaps more importantly, all three involve the loss of freedom: freedom to have what we please, control whom we please, and do what we please. In poverty, obscurity, and humility, we are forced to surrender to someone else's will, like wild animals hunted down and trapped for the zoo. Or so it seems to those on the outside looking in. For others, who have chosen those paths out of joyful obedience, the door to freedom has been flung wide open.

It's a concept few of us understand.

Neither does Éowyn—at first.

She is a "daughter of kings," born to lead, bred to rule. True, she is willing to let others take center stage, but only those whom she deems worthy, including Théoden and Aragorn, and only if she can play Best Supporting Actress. As Faramir so astutely points out, she has loved Aragorn "because he was high and puissant, and [she] wished to have renown and glory and to be lifted far above the mean things that crawl on the earth."[15] Ouch.

Éowyn believes that she is born for greatness. And this is not far from the truth. But her definition of greatness is nothing less than to be queen of Middle-earth—she will settle for no other path in life. Even after playing a starring role in defeating the king of the Ringwraiths—a great and glorious deed if ever there was one—she is still restless, haunting the walls of Minas Tirith in hopes of news from the battlefront, pacing the cage of her own soul. When first confronted with the master plan of what her future holds, she refuses to accept it, thinking that an alternative course—one of her own choosing—will be the key to freedom.

At the heart of this behavior is the fear of obscurity: that one's name and deeds will be erased from living memory, before one's life is even over. Obscurity . . . the daily grind of service in a job for which one is overqualified and underappreciated; the overlooked nameplate on the door of some forgotten nursing home; the lonely question "Who?" in the reading of an obituary. To finish one's days having contributed nothing of substance to the course of human history—that is the obscure life.

We are all born for greatness—or so our parents and teachers and coaches tell us. And that is true, to some degree. We were all made for a reason, with unique gifts and talents and skills that God wants to use to help make the world a better place. In time, as we align ourselves with God's Master Plan, our sense of identity and purpose becomes clearer and clearer. The problem is, we want greatness on our own terms, rather than on God's terms. We're not willing to allow him to prescribe our path or to use us in the ways that he sees fit. If God doesn't place us where we think he should, with the "right" kinds of people or doing the "right" kinds of things, then we begin to pace the cage of our souls, restless.

Yet more often than not, God's people *are* called to do things that seem pretty obscure. We're asked to care for aging grandparents or work behind the scenes in dead-end jobs or pound hammers on mission trips or change diapers or wash load after load of laundry till we never want to see another sock. Each of these might feel like a "small matter in the great deeds of this time,"[16] but in God's perspective, they are important details in the ongoing plot of history, without which the story could never unfold.

Think back to Jesus' parable. The rich lord commends the two good servants by saying, "Well done, good and faithful servant! You have been faithful with a few things; I will put you in charge of many things. Come and share your master's happiness!" (Matthew 25:21). Not only do the small, daily drudgeries count in the Master Plan, but there is tremendous joy to be found in the doing of them! We are freed from the bondage of our fears, able to relax without the burden of greatness on our shoulders, content with leaving the course of events up to God's providential control.

When Éowyn finally relinquishes her need to have greatness on her own terms, she is free to love Faramir, free to serve the people in her care, free to pursue her true calling as a "healer" rather than a warrior queen.

This is the lesson of Éowyn, pacing the walls of Minas Tirith with Faramir at her side:

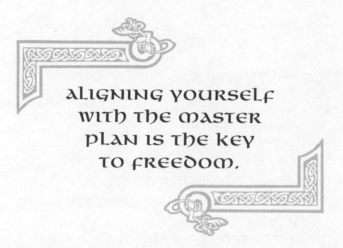

ALIGNING YOURSELF WITH THE MASTER PLAN IS THE KEY TO FREEDOM.

So what are you going to do about it?

It is for freedom that Christ has set us free. Stand firm, then, and do not let yourselves be burdened again by a yoke of slavery.
GALATIANS 5:1

THE WORD ON FREEDOM

Take some time to read one or more of the following Bible passages:
Psalm 118:5-6; John 8:32, 34-36; Romans 6:20-22; 2 Corinthians 3:17; Galatians 4:1-7; 5:13; 1 Peter 2:16

GOING FURTHER:

Why do people fear obscurity?

In what ways do you dream of greatness?

When have you been asked to do something that you felt was too obscure to really matter in the grand scheme of life? How did you (or do you) feel?

What evidence have you seen that there is freedom (and joy!) in doing what God has planned for you, however small the task?

What are you going to do about it?

WEEK EIGHT

CHOOSING
CONTROL
or
SERVANTHOOD

Part One:

CHOOSING CONTROL

"As the Power grows, its proved friends will also grow; and the Wise, such as you and I, may with patience come at last to direct its courses, to control it."

—SARUMAN TO GANDALF, FROM *THE FELLOWSHIP OF THE RING,* BOOK TWO, CHAPTER TWO

Saruman, too, seeks greatness. But unlike Éowyn, who desires what she cannot have, he has been given it freely, appointed for the task.

The members of the Council of the Wise, which include Gandalf, Galadriel, Elrond, and others, have chosen Saruman the White to lead them, despite Galadriel's protests that Gandalf is the better leader. Saruman proves faithful at first, guiding them through many difficult decisions and using his position to serve those under his care. He even takes on the responsibility of studying the One Ring, to research its lore and its power, to discern Sauron's motives, and to possibly locate the Ring before Sauron can. But soon Saruman, like so many others, becomes corrupted by the promise of ultimate power. Soon his only motive is to exercise dominion and control over all the creatures of Middle-earth, including those who have put their trust in him.

So why don't the Wise (everyone except Galadriel, that is) catch on sooner? It's not that Saruman is all that powerful or impressive. Even his voice, though eloquent and enchanting, doesn't exercise the same kind of control over the Council that it does on the masses. No, his real strength lies in his very familiarity. The Wise know him as a friend and colleague. He has proven himself trustworthy, having earned their love and allegiance over time. Up to this point, he has used his leadership only to serve the folk of Middle-earth, as he was sent to do. What reason do they have now to doubt him?

Were a known emissary of Sauron to come before the Council and make the suggestions that Saruman does, the Wise would not be so easily swayed. They would hear every word with guarded suspicion, no matter how eloquent the presentation, and quickly discern the sneaky agenda behind the deal. But because Saruman is known and trusted, he can manipulate the discussions and decisions just as he pleases without anyone being aware. He abuses that trust right up to the moment when he discovers the location of the Ring. Then he unveils his true purpose with hateful abandon. And as Gandalf reflects, "Nothing that we have endured of late has seemed so grievous as the treason of Isengard."[17]

Few of us could be accused of such wicked ambition. But all of us have hurt the ones who know us and love us best, including our parents, siblings, friends, and roommates.

As Lord Chesterfield said, "Most people enjoy the inferiority of their friends."[18] It's a control issue. The more others look up to us, the more influence we can have over them so they will do what we want. By the same token, it's so very simple to take for granted the love and attention of our family members. We forget that love is a free gift of grace from God—not something that we earn or deserve—and we begin to interact with them as if they are serfs above whom we are lords and ladies.

If we're honest, we find these people pretty useful. Our parents will bend over backwards to make us happy—a useful quality when we want something that only they can afford to get us. Our siblings share some of those same wants—a useful quality when heavy artillery is needed to convince the parents. Our roommates and friends have any number of things (CDs, clothes, cars) that we like to borrow. The more control we can exercise over them, the more useful they become.

Jesus has fairly harsh words for such behavior. The Pharisees are his favorite example. Not only are they spiritually proud, but they enjoy the special attention of the masses, which they use to their advantage. But Jesus blows the whistle on them: "Woe to you Pharisees, because you love the most important seats in the synagogues and greetings in the marketplaces" (Luke 11:43). *Woe* is not a word he uses lightly. He's saying, in essence, "Prepare for destruction." What goes around, comes around.

Occasionally our loved ones get wise to what we're doing and call us to account. But most of the time, if we're really subtle, they never catch on until we've hurt them severely.

This is the lesson of Saruman, abusing the trust of those in his care:

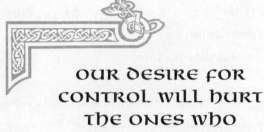

OUR DESIRE FOR CONTROL WILL HURT THE ONES WHO LOVE US BEST.

So what are you going to do about it?

Jesus called them together and said, "You know that the rulers of the Gentiles lord it over them, and their high officials exercise authority over them. Not so with you."
MATTHEW 20:25-26

THE WORD ON CONTROL

Take some time to read one or more of the following Bible passages:
Matthew 23:1-7; Luke 14:7-11; 2 Corinthians 1:24; Titus 3:1-2; 1 Peter 5:1-3; Jude 1:16-19

GOING FURTHER:

What is it like to have a really controlling friend or family member?

How does it feel when a family member or friend treats you as if you're merely "useful"?

In what ways do you treat others that way?

In what ways do you tend to take their love for granted?

What are you going to do about it?

Part Two:

CHOOSING SERVANTHOOD

"Do you really mean that Strider is one of the people of the old Kings?" said Frodo in wonder. "I thought they had all vanished long ago. I thought he was only a Ranger."
–FROM *THE FELLOWSHIP OF THE RING*, BOOK TWO, CHAPTER ONE

If there is any character who is called to greatness, it is Aragorn, son of Arathorn, heir to the throne

of Gondor. He, like Saruman, is given the responsibility of leadership by the Wise, who have known
his true identity and destiny since his birth. He is
the one for whom the people of Middle-earth
have been waiting many long centuries. But instead of using that position to further his own
ambitions or desires, he seems to prefer obscurity—as if he has no personal ambitions at all.

In fact, when Frodo first encounters him at the inn
in Bree, Aragorn has spent the bulk of his adult life
as an unknown Ranger named Strider, protecting
the borders of the Shire (and elsewhere) from the
Enemy. The Hobbits haven't even known such
folk existed—that the Shire owes its uninterrupted
centuries of peace to these brave men. But that's
just how Strider likes it. The less people know
about him, the better he is able to serve them. So
when called upon to lead this little band of
Hobbits from Bree to Rivendell, he sees it as
merely an extension of what he has been doing all
along: caring for the needs of his people.

And so it continues, book after book, page after

page. He leads the Fellowship after Gandalf's fall in Moria—pausing when they need to rest, driving them on when their safety is threatened, snatching sleep for himself only when absolutely necessary. Then, when the Fellowship dissolves and the War of the Ring begins, he marches in the front lines, putting himself at risk time and time again in order to secure victory. And when called upon to heal the wounded, as is his kingly gift, he still will not reveal his true identity until the people of Gondor are ready to receive him.

Even after Strider is finally revealed (to the astonishment of the Hobbits) as the one true king, nothing changes in his demeanor or ambitions. Aragorn still leads in order to serve, as will be his mission until the end of his days.

And so it is ours.

Though not all of us will be called to lead, all of us are called to love and serve others—a concept that is almost cliché in Christian circles. And at first glance, it appears to be a fairly simple assignment—

if we talk in terms of "those poor people" (mostly nameless and faceless) who live so far away, to whom we send money and canned goods and old coats. But it becomes a bit harder when we talk in terms of those to whom we are nearest: our parents, siblings, dormmates, or friends.

We belong to these people. They have certain claims on us that cannot be ignored without serious turmoil in our domestic lives. And it's not just a matter of treating them with respect, like our colleagues or acquaintances. No, it's about considering them *better* than ourselves (Philippians 2:3). *Their* needs come first before our own. Our minds constantly dwell on what *they* would want, what *their* day must have been like, what life might look like from *their* perspective. And then we act accordingly.

Think about it in terms of coming in the door after a long day of school or work. What's the first thing on your mind? What's your goal for the evening? Now imagine that, before you even get close to home, your mind is already beginning to dwell on those who will be there. You've already started to ask yourself, *What do I know about Mom's day today? What kinds of things would my brother like to talk about? What would my roommate like to do? How can I be helpful to my dad?*

Sound cheesy? Try doing it. Not only will it rigorously test your character, but it also will completely bewilder the ones you're trying to serve. Your mom may look at you with suspicion, wondering if this is the antecedent to yet another request for funds. Your roommate may think this is perhaps one of your more interesting passive-aggressive ploys to avoid cleaning the toilet. Your brother may follow you down the hall trying to pick a quarrel—out of sheer curiosity. But still you plod on, like Strider leading a band of grumbling Hobbits from Bree to Rivendell. *Their* needs come first, every step of the way.

Jesus said, "For even the Son of Man did not come to be served, but to serve, and to give his life as a ransom for many" (Mark 10:45). Greatness is not about bending others to your will, like Saruman tried to do, but bending your will toward others. Servanthood is the true test of character, the mark of royalty on those who belong to the King.

Such is the lesson of Aragorn, putting the needs of the Fellowship before his own:

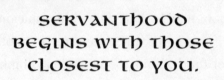

SERVANTHOOD BEGINS WITH THOSE CLOSEST TO YOU.

So what are you going to do about it?

For even the Son of Man did not come to be served, but to serve, and to give his life as a ransom for many. MARK 10:45

THE WORD ON SERVANTHOOD

Take some time to read one or more of the following Bible passages:
Matthew 23:11; Mark 10:43-45; Luke 22:27; Philippians 2:3-11; 2 Timothy 2:24-25

GOING FURTHER:

When you hear the word *servanthood,* what comes to mind?

How easy or difficult is it to serve those closest to you: your parents, siblings, roommates, or friends?

What are some practical ways you can put their needs before your own?

What might be the possible outcome—and why is that worth it?

What are you going to do about it?

WEEK NINE

CHOOSING
DESPAIR
or
HOPE

Part One:

choosing despair

To the air he had returned, summoning his steed ere the darkness failed, and now he was come again, bringing ruin, turning hope to despair, and victory to death.

—On the Captain of the Nazgûl, from *The Return of the King*, Book Five, Chapter Six

The nearer Frodo and Sam get to Mount Doom, the more we realize just how close a shave they had back in the Shire. It's amazing to think that at least one Ringwraith made it to the very threshold of Bag End, only to find that its occupants had just left—and that the Hobbits were tracked to within inches of their hiding place in the woods. It isn't until they meet Strider in Bree, who apprises them of *what* exactly has been on their trail, that they begin to understand just how vulnerable they are. And it isn't until the skirmish at Weathertop, where Frodo is wounded, that they realize their true helplessness.

For against these ghosts there is no apparent defense. The Ringwraiths, or Nazgûl, are the spirits of ancient kings, kept "alive" by their lust for power and their enslavement to the One Ring. Even Sauron's own hosts are terrified of them; the Orcs would "slay themselves" at the Nazgûl's bidding. Despite their temporary setback at the ford near Rivendell, where the horses are drowned in the sudden flood, the Ringwraiths soon return, mounted on winged steeds and more horrible than ever.

As Sauron's malice grows, so does the terrifying effect of the Nazgûl's cries, echoing over the walls of Minas Tirith in Gondor. "Stouthearted" Men drop to the ground in fear while others stand paralyzed, "letting their weapons fall from nerveless hands while into their minds a blackness [comes], and they [think] no more of war, but only of hiding and of crawling, and of death."[19] Then, after the Nazgûl pass, the Men are filled with shame at their own weakness. Their inability to stand firm is yet another torment in what has become Sauron's preemptive strike—a psychological attack before the real battle begins.

Yet it's not even the terror of the Nazgûl that overwhelms these Men. It's the emptiness and powerlessness of their own souls. In trying to summon any amount of courage or character to stand bravely against the threat, they discover that they have none. They can do nothing.

It's a spiritual experience we all face, at one time or another. Despite the accolades of our parents and teachers, despite the reality that we are unconditionally loved by a loving Creator, we all face the moment in which we realize that we can, in fact, do nothing. It's a terrifying experience.

Strangely enough, the crisis often happens in the midst of devotion, prayer, and self-examination. As we read God's Word and ask ourselves the tough questions, we begin to realize more and more our own weakness. The twentieth-century monk Thomas Merton put it this way: "Sometimes prayer, meditation, and contemplation are 'death'— a kind of descent into our own nothingness, a recognition of helplessness, frustration, infidelity, confusion, ignorance." We are like the prophet Isaiah in the presence of the seraphim: "I am ruined! For I am a man of unclean lips, and I live among a people of unclean lips" (Isaiah 6:5).

At every great turning point, every great crisis, there is that "descent into our own nothingness." Our masks and facades are stripped away and our naked souls come face-to-face with the truth. It is only after we look inside ourselves and see the vast chasm of our own emptiness, the huge abyss of sin,

that we find ourselves crying out for Someone—
Someone higher and holier—to heal the breach, to
fill us with a life far better than we could ever manage on our own. This is a moment of true confes-
sion, leading either to despair or to new life.

Jesus said, "I am the vine; you are the branches. . . .
apart from me you can do nothing" (John 15:5).
Unfortunately, we too often become focused on
the "nothing" and forget the "apart from me." We
forget that we belong to Christ. In him we are
something and *someone!* The moment we realize
that truth, we can turn from the "descent into
nothingness" and begin the long climb up and out.

There are moments of "nothingness" all throughout *The Lord of the Rings,* when the characters need
help from a power outside themselves. Théoden
and his men make their last ride into the battle at
Helm's Deep. Éowyn faces the Captain of the
Nazgûl in hand-to-hand combat. The good forces
of Middle-earth look up from the battlefield to see
the dreaded ships sailing up the Anduin. Frodo
and Sam stumble down the slopes of Mount

Doom, the earth disintegrating beneath their feet. In each situation the key players are convinced that their next step will be their last. They have done all that is possible on their own strength. They must get help from others—or perish.

This is the lesson of the Ringwraiths, circling over the walls of Minas Tirith:

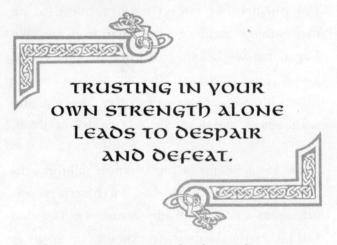

TRUSTING IN YOUR OWN STRENGTH ALONE LEADS TO DESPAIR AND DEFEAT.

So what are you going to do about it?

The enemy pursues me, he crushes me to the ground; he makes me dwell in darkness like those long dead. So

my spirit grows faint within me; my heart within me is dismayed.
PSALM 143:3-4

THE WORD ON DESPAIR

Take some time to read one or more of the following Bible passages:
Psalm 42:5; 142; 143; Matthew 27:45-46;
2 Corinthians 1:8-11

GOING FURTHER:

What is the true source of despair?

When (if ever) have you experienced despair? What is it like?

When (if ever) have you experienced the "descent into nothingness"—when you realized you needed God's help?

Who do you know who is experiencing despair right now?

What are you going to do about it?

Part Two:

choosing hope

"The Eagles are coming! The Eagles are coming!"
—From *The Return of the King*, Book Five, Chapter Ten

If our journey with Frodo has made anything clear, it's to not trust appearances. We've been "burned" more than once by the deceptive natures of characters like Saruman, Wormtongue, and Denethor.

We've learned not to get *too* attached to anything or anyone; much that "once was" is now lost forever. We've gotten used to funerals. We're surprised at nothing anymore. As Frodo and Sam stumble down the side of Mount Doom, hopelessly caught in the midst of that erupting volcano, we're tempted to think, *So this is it, after all. I should have known better than to get too involved.*

At the same time, something else inside us says, *It'll be worth it, I promise!* Perhaps we've gotten a hint of the ending from our *LOTR*-junkie friends. After all, this is supposed to be *the good stuff.* Or maybe we've figured that no one would sink that many years—or that many millions of dollars—into something that is a colossal bummer.

Yet more likely, we've begun to trust that Tolkien will not let us down.

It's a strange relationship, that of reader and author. As readers, we have some sense of an author's purpose and direction, but we're never quite sure he'll pull through on his promises. After all, the author's not really responsible to us (is he?). We don't know if his story will end in comedy (a word that originally meant "happy ending") or tragedy. But if we've stuck it out this long, shouldn't we be rewarded somehow? Can't the author intervene and do something really inspiring that will make it all seem worth it?

And yet Tolkien does so, time and time again. When Théoden and the rest ride to certain death in the battle at Helm's Deep, they are met instead by the figure of Gandalf coming to their rescue—with a host of troops behind him. When Éowyn faces off with the Captain of the Nazgûl, Merry finds a sudden strength beyond all strength to help her. When the good forces of Middle-earth look up in horror at the advancing enemy ships, they see to their astonishment that the lead ship is in fact flying the standard of Arwen, with Aragorn on board.

So when the Eagles appear at "the end of all things" to rescue Frodo and Sam from the foot of Mount Doom, we really should not be surprised.

Having made it this close to the closing credits and the final pages, we should have prepared ourselves for something exceptionally good. But for some reason we still cling to our seats, white-knuckled, afraid that Tolkien will withhold from us this last little bit of joy, our last and only hope.

Too often we treat God with the same mistrust.

Despite the fact that the Author of life has promised a happy ending, we still seem to think he will plan something awful along the way. After all, suffering is a major plot device in most great stories: that's how the characters—we—develop and change. In the midst of suffering it's desperately hard to see the happy ending. We begin to question the Author's intentions. If things are this bad now, why should we harbor any hopes they'll improve?

Some people use the issue of suffering as their biggest argument against the existence of a loving, all-powerful God. How could such a Being allow horrible things to happen to us? Yet if we apply that same logic to a book and its author, we hit some major roadblocks. Just because the characters in a book experience pain and loss does not mean that the author either *(a)* doesn't care, or *(b)* can't control the plot, or *(c)* doesn't actually exist in the first place. While *c* is obviously *not* true, in most instances of really bad writing either *a* or *b* is true. But not so with *the good stuff.* In that case, the author has a reason for what's happening. Suffering has a purpose.

The apostle Paul said that "we know that suffering produces perseverance; perseverance, character; and character, hope. And hope does not disappoint us" (Romans 5:3-5). The Author of the story does not leave us to our own devices, to fail miserably after suffering valiantly at his command. He intervenes—sometimes at the last possible moment—to save us, and promises a happy ending beyond anything we could imagine!

The great story of Scripture is full of God's promises. God says he will never leave us nor forsake us (Joshua 1:5). Jesus says he will be with us always

(Matthew 28:20). The apostle John sees a vision of heaven in which there is no more "night," no pain, no death; in which God wipes away every tear from our eyes (Revelation 21:4 and 22:5). It is in this that we put our hope: not in our own strength or ability to choose the right thing for the right reasons, but in God, the Author of the story, the original inventor of all *good stuff.*

So this journey with Frodo has been worth it, after all! We've seen evidence that all our choices, though murky and difficult now, have significance in the great battle between darkness and light. It's clear that when the Author of the story promises something, he means it. We can trust that in the darkest hour, when all seems hopeless, help "unlooked for" is on its way.

This is the lesson of the Eagles, arriving at the last possible moment to save Frodo and Sam from the foot of Mount Doom:

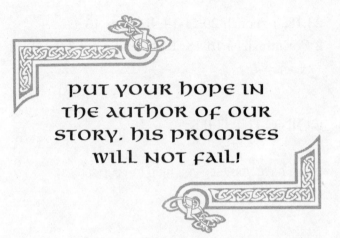

PUT YOUR HOPE IN THE AUTHOR OF OUR STORY, HIS PROMISES WILL NOT FAIL!

So what are you going to do about it?

Even youths grow tired and weary, and young men stumble and fall; but those who hope in the Lord will renew their strength. They will soar on wings like eagles; they will run and not grow weary, they will walk and not be faint.
ISAIAH 40:30-31

THE WORD ON HOPE

Take some time to read one or more of the following Bible passages:
Deuteronomy 31:6; Psalm 121; 130; Proverbs

23:18; Jeremiah 29:11-14; Romans 15:4;
2 Corinthians 4:16-18; 1 Thessalonians 1:3

GOING FURTHER:

When have you received help in your darkest
moments?

When have you been able to look back on a bad
situation and see *the good stuff* God has done
through it?

How can you better trust that God, the Author of
your life, will make good on his promises?

What sort of happy ending does God promise for
those who faithfully walk with Jesus?

What are you going to do about it?

Let us fix our eyes on Jesus, the author and perfecter of our faith.

HEBREWS 12:2

ENДNOTES

[1] Humphrey Carpenter, *The Letters of J. R. R. Tolkien* (New York: Houghton Mifflin Company, 2000), 199.

[2] J. R. R. Tolkien, *The Return of the King* (New York: Ballantine Books, 1965), 28.

[3] Computer-Generated Images

[4] J. R. R. Tolkien, *The Fellowship of the Ring* (New York: Ballantine Books, 1965), 428.

[5] Ibid., 428.

[6] Ibid., 429.

[7] Ibid., 432.

[8] J. R. R. Tolkien, *The Two Towers* (New York: Ballantine Books, 1965), 127.

[9] G. K. Chesterton was a Christian apologist and writer from the early twentieth century, much admired by Tolkien and his friends.

[10] Tolkien, *King*, 249.

[11] Tolkien, *Fellowship*, 335.

[12] Ibid., 461.

[13] Dietrich Bonhoeffer, *Letters and Papers from Prison*, ed. Eberhard Bethge (New York: Macmillan Publishing Co., 1971), 14.

[14] Tolkien, *Towers*, 156.

[15] Tolkien, *King*, 299.

[16] Tolkien, *Towers,* 33.

[17] Ibid., 128.

[18] Lord Chesterfield was an eighteenth-century British politician.

[19] Tolkien, *King,* 118.

QUICK REFERENCE GUIDE: A GLOSSARY OF TERMS

for Those Who Have Never Read the Books

(My apologies to *The Silmarillion* fans. There simply isn't room for extended background information. These are just the basics.)

Anduin The great river that cuts through the kingdom of Gondor in the east of Middle-earth.

Aragorn The secret heir to the throne of Gondor. As "Strider," he leads the band of Hobbits from the Shire to Rivendell.

Arwen Elrond's daughter, the Elven fiancée of Aragorn.

Bag End Bilbo's home in the Shire, inherited by his cousin Frodo.

Balrog A powerful, demonic creature from deep in the Mines of Moria. He attacks the Fellowship and causes Gandalf to fall.

Benji the Brave A completely made-up character who has nothing to do with *The Lord of the Rings*.

Bilbo The first Hobbit (or Halfling) to encounter the Ring, star of Tolkien's *The Hobbit*. He gives the Ring to his cousin Frodo.

Bodysurf A postmodern form of self-expression in which a sweaty person relies on the kindness and stupidity of strangers to physically pass him over the heads of a moshing crowd. See *Mosh*.

Boromir The eldest son of Lord Denethor, Steward of Gondor. He joins the Fellowship at Rivendell but can't resist the tempting power of the Ring.

Bree The village on the edge of the Shire where both Men and Hobbits dwell. The Prancing Pony Inn is there, where the Hobbits meet Strider/Aragorn for the first time.

CGI Computer-Generated Images.

Council of the Wise Consisting of Gandalf, Galadriel, Elrond, and others who advise the good creatures of Middle-earth in their ongoing battle against Sauron. Representatives of their respective peoples meet in Rivendell to determine the fate of the Ring.

Dark Lord See *Sauron*.

Denethor The Steward of Gondor in the city of Minas Tirith; father of Boromir and Faramir. He secretly possesses one of the "seeing stones." (Saruman and Sauron each have one also.) See *Seeing Stones*.

Dwarves Man-like characters, shorter and generally tougher, who prefer to live underground; they have a long-standing feud with the Elves.

Eagles Enormous birds that seem to work for the "good side" of Middle-earth; they always show up when there's no hope left.

Elrond The Master of Rivendell, who hosts the Council of the Ring; the half-elven father of Arwen.

Elves The firstborn among the created beings of Middle-earth; they are immortal and have a curious ability to discern the thoughts of others. They have a long-standing feud with the Dwarves.

Ents Treelike creatures that are called the Shepherds of the Forest; they dwell in the forest of Fangorn and befriend Merry and Pippin.

Éomer Loyal nephew of King Théoden of Rohan.

Éowyn Sister of Éomer, loyal niece to King Théoden of Rohan.

Fangorn A large and mysterious forest that few travelers dare enter; it is home to the Ents.

Faramir The youngest son of Denethor of Gondor and younger brother of Boromir. He encounters Frodo and Sam at Henneth Annûn near the borders of

Mordor, where he resists the temptation to possess the Ring for Gondor.

Fellowship The Fellowship of the Ring; the nine representatives of "good" Middle-earth who set out from Rivendell to destroy the Ring in the fires of Mount Doom in Mordor: Gandalf, Aragorn, Boromir, Legolas, Gimli, Frodo, Sam, Merry, and Pippin.

Frodo The main Hobbit hero of *The Lord of the Rings*. Once he learns that Bilbo's Ring must be taken into Mordor and destroyed, he volunteers to take it, though it means possibly leaving behind the Shire forever.

Galadriel The Queen of the Elves of Lothlórien.

Gandalf The good Wizard who guides the Fellowship from Rivendell into the Mines of Moria, where he is lost fighting the Balrog. He returns later to help win the War of the Ring.

Gimli The only Dwarf to travel with the Fellowship from Rivendell; he becomes best friends with Legolas the Elf.

Gollum Also called *Sméagol;* an ancient corrupted Hobbit who once possessed the Ring before it ended up with Bilbo. In trying to get the Ring back, he finds and follows Frodo and Sam, eventually becoming their guide into Mordor.

Gondor A kingdom of Men in southeast Middle-earth. Stewards have ruled it for centuries until the line of kings can be restored. Aragorn is the secret heir to the throne.

Haldir One of the chief Elven guards of Lothlórien.

Helm's Deep The location of the fortress from which the Riders of Rohan make their stand against the Wizard Saruman. See *Rohan.*

Henneth Annûn The secret hideout of Faramir and his men of Gondor, hidden by a waterfall near the border of Mordor.

Hobbits Also called Halflings; small people from the Shire in the northwestern part of Middle-earth, often mistaken for children of Men.

Horn of Ippydoo A completely made-up thing that has nothing to do with *The Lord of the Rings.*

Isildur Aragorn's ancestor, who cut the Ring from Sauron's finger and then failed to destroy it in Mount Doom.

Isengard The fortress of the Wizard Saruman.

Khazad-dûm The Dwarvish name for the Mines of Moria.

Legolas The only Elf to travel with the Fellowship from Rivendell; he becomes best friends with Gimli the Dwarf.

Lothlórien The woods where the Elven queen

Galadriel lives. The Fellowship flees there after escaping the Mines of Moria.

LOTR-**Induced Depressive Disorder (*LOTR*-IDD)** A completely fictional psychological disorder brought about by subjecting oneself to high doses of depressing scenes from *The Lord of the Rings*.

LOTR **junkies** *The Lord of the Rings* fanatics who host their own fan Web sites, speak both dialects of Elvish, and know how to beat all eighty-six thousand levels of the computer game.

Merry One of the Hobbits who joins the Fellowship; a cousin and close friend of Frodo's from the Shire.

Middle-earth The imaginary land in which most of *The Lord of the Rings* story takes place.

Minas Tirith The capital city of Gondor.

Mordor The land seized by Sauron, the Dark Lord, for his kingdom. It is in the east of Middle-earth.

Moria The Elvish word for the ancient underground kingdom of the Dwarves; also called the Mines of Moria. This is where Gandalf fights the Balrog and falls into the abyss.

Mork A completely made-up character who has nothing to do with *The Lord of the Rings* but has everything to do with a nutty sitcom from the late seventies.

Mosh A postmodern form of aggressive self-expression in which crowds of sweaty people deliberately smash into each other and somehow manage not to take it personally. It has nothing to do with *The Lord of the Rings* (unless you count the battle at Helm's Deep).

Mount Doom Where the Ring was forged, in the very heart of Mordor.

Nazgûl The nine Ringwraiths, or Ring Lords, that are the main generals in Sauron's army. They are basically ghosts kept alive by their lust for the One Ring.

Orcs The employees of Sauron. They were once Elves but became corrupted.

Orthanc Saruman's tower at Isengard, where Gandalf is trapped for many days.

Pippin One of the Hobbits who joins the Fellowship; a close friend of Frodo's from the Shire.

Ranger Aragorn and other descendants of the ancient kings who "secretly" serve Middle-earth as its protectors.

Ring The One Ring made by Sauron to control all the other Rings of Power. It was lost for many centuries until it was found by Gollum, who kept it for a few centuries until it was found by Bilbo. It is finally given to Bilbo's cousin Frodo, who sets out with the Fellowship to destroy the Ring in Mount Doom in Mordor.

Ringwraiths See *Nazgûl.*

Rivendell The House of Elrond, where the Council meets to decide what will be done with the Ring. From there the Fellowship sets out for Mordor.

Rohan The Kingdom of Riders, or Rohirrim (the horse people), near the center of Middle-earth, close to Isengard.

Samwise Gamgee (Sam) Frodo's loyal gardener from the Shire, who vows to stick by his master to the bitter end.

Saruman A Wizard colleague of Gandalf's who becomes corrupted; he wants the Ring for himself. Saruman sends his hosts to fight King Théoden in the battle at Helm's Deep.

Sauron The main bad guy in *The Lord of the Rings*. After the Elves formed the first Rings of Power long ago, Sauron forged the One Ring to control them all. But the Ring has become lost, and he is trying to find it. Once he knows that a Hobbit of the Shire has it, the War of the Ring begins.

Seeing Stones Also called the *palantir;* "magic" stones once used by Men to see what was going on in the world and to communicate with one another. Saruman, Sauron, and Denethor each have one.

Shelob The giant spider that lives in a series of tunnels on the border of Mordor.

Shire, The The homeland of the Hobbits.

Silmarillion, The Tolkien's comprehensive history and mythology of Middle-earth.

Sméagol See *Gollum.*

Steward of Gondor See *Denethor.*

Strider See *Aragorn.*

Théoden The aging king of Rohan; he has been under the spell of Saruman (thanks to the influence of the treacherous counselor Wormtongue). Once freed, he joins forces with the rest of Middle-earth to fight both Saruman and Sauron.

Tolkien, J. R. R. Author of *The Lord of the Rings, The Hobbit,* and *The Silmarillion.*

Uruk-hai The Orc-like henchmen created by Saruman; they possess the ability to travel by day as well as by night (unlike the Orcs, who can only travel by night).

War of the Ring Sauron's last pitch to try and wrest the Ring from the good forces of Middle-earth.

Weathertop The high hill where Frodo is wounded by the Ringwraiths.

Wizards Powerful Man-like characters sent to defend Middle-earth from Sauron. Among them are Saruman and Gandalf.

Wormtongue The traitorous counselor of King Théoden of Rohan; he is actually working for the Wizard Saruman.

COMING FALL 2003

Sammy's dead . . .
they each played a part.
Kyra, his twin sister;
Miranda, the girl he loved; and
Tyrone, a friend from school.

What's the real story?

Three novels that walk through real life and real issues—
there's always more than one point of view.

Kyra's Story, by Dandi Daley Mackall
Miranda's Story, by Melody Carlson
Tyrone's Story, by Sigmund Brouwer

Go to www.thirstybooks.com for more info